An Interactive
Learner Journal

English Reflections

Andrew Finch

Second Edition, plus
Socratic Dialogs and
Discussions

Foreword to the second edition

Welcome to English Reflections!

This journal is an English textbook, a personal diary, a learning journal, and a collection of integrated, interactive, reflective activities. Its purpose is to raise awareness of the learning process, while fostering self-confidence, motivation, and autonomous learning. Interactive reflection on educational ideas helps us to refine those ideas and to adapt teaching practices to the needs of the most important people in the classroom - the learners.

This journal has two focuses:

1. **Interaction:** This involves listening, sharing, and growing together, and is a crucial aspect of language learning. This journal contains interactive questionnaires, surveys, discussion topics, and other activities which encourage everyone to talk, listen, read and write about learning. These activities are performed best in the classroom.
2. **Reflection:** This includes thinking about learning needs, learning strategies, learning achievements, and future study plans. It includes reflection on feelings, observations and opinions about learning. In this book, reflections are written in the My Reflections pages, where individual opinions about learning can be expressed, based on and enhanced by the group discussions and interactions of the preceding pages.

As we reflect on the issues in this journal, unconscious learning processes will be activated, and a new perspective on learning and life will grow inside us - a perspective of language learning as education of the whole person - intellect, feelings, emotions, and social skills. We will see that education is about learning how to learn and how to activate cognitive, affective, social and linguistic learning strategies.

Learning how to learn is life's most important skill. (Tony Buzan)

If we respect ourselves as learners, if we trust ourselves as responsible human beings and if we have the skills to control what we learn and how we learn it, we will discover an invaluable treasure - the love of learning. This will serve us forever, helping us to learn new skills, take on new ideas, and adapt to new situations. Such a love of learning functions best in a non-threatening learning environment, allowing learners to progress from the warm-hearted interaction of the classroom to untold and unimagined learning experiences in their future lives.

Develop a passion for learning. If you do,
you will never cease to grow. (Anthony D'Angelo)

This book is dedicated to Heebon, my wife,
for her insightful comments,
for her invaluable understanding,
and for being there in peace and love.

Contents: 1

Section	*Title*	*Pages*
Opening	Foreword	1
	Contents	2-3
	Weekly Planner	4
	Semester Planner	5
	Ideas for My Reflections	6
Personal discovery 1	Personal Profile	7
	Self-Assessment (What can we do now?)	8
	Ideas that are Important to Me	9
	Star Signs	10
	My Reflections 1	11
Personal discovery 2	Autonomy and Self-Direction	12-13
	Multiple Intelligences Survey (MIS)	14-17
	Discussion (Education)	18
	My Reflections 2	19
Needs analysis	Needs Analysis (Who wants to ...?)	20
	Self-Assessment (My learning)	21
	Students' Needs	22
	Teachers' Needs	23
	Discussion (Learning goals)	24-25
	My Reflections 3	26
Learning styles	Our Learning Preferences	27
	Study Habits (True or false?)	28-29
	Learning-Style Inventory (LSI)	30-31
	Discussion (Our learning styles)	32
	My Reflections 4	33
Beliefs and perceptions	Beliefs About Language Learning (BALLI)	34
	My Perceptions about Learning	35
	Stereotypes	36-37
	Discussion (Language Learning ideas)	38
	My Reflections 5	39
Study skills	Study Skills: Memory	40-41
	Study Skills Interview	42
	Self-Assessment (Motivation)	43
	Learner-Counseling Role-Play (1)	44
	My Reflections 6	45
Feedback 1	Peer Feedback (Classmate's Thoughts)	46

Contents: 2

Section	Title	Pages
Learning environment	Classroom Learning Environment (CLE)	47
	Classroom Questionnaire 1 (CEQ preferred)	48
	Classroom Questionnaire 2 (CEQ actual)	49
	Classroom Environment Scale (CES)	50
	Self-Assessment (Participation)	51
	Pre-Nuptial Agreement (Contract 1)	52
	My Reflections 7	53
Affect	A Good Thing	54
	Foreign Language Classroom Anxiety Scale (FLCAS)	55
	Discussion (Lifestyles)	56-57
	Self-Assessment (Confidence)	58
	My Reflections 8	59
Learning strategies	Strategy Inventory (SILL)	60-64
	Call My Bluff	65-66
	Learner-Counseling Role Play (2)	67
	Discussion (Learning to learn)	68
	My Reflections 9	69
Collaboration	What Should I Do?	70
	Share the Wealth	71
	Learning Contract (Contract 2)	72
	Learner-Counseling Role Play (3)	73
	My Reflections 10	74
CALL/MALL	Computer Assisted Language Learning (CALL)	75
	CALL/MALL Board Game	76
	Software for the Language Classroom	77
	Discussion (The Internet and language learning)	78
	My Reflections 11	79
Reflections	Self-Assessment (Language functions)	80-81
	Highlights of My Life	82-83
	Final Contract (Contract 3)	84
	Review, Discussion & Letter to Myself	85
	My Reflections 12	86
Feedback 2	What Did I Learn?	87
	Teacher Feedback (Teacher's Thoughts)	88
Further reflections	Socratic Dialogs and Discussions	89-117

My Weekly Planner

	Monday	Tuesday	Wednesday	Thursday	Friday	Saturday	Sunday
8 am							
9 am							
10 am							
11 am							
12 pm							
1 pm							
2 pm							
3 pm							
4 pm							
5 pm							
6 pm							
7 pm							
8 pm							
9 pm							

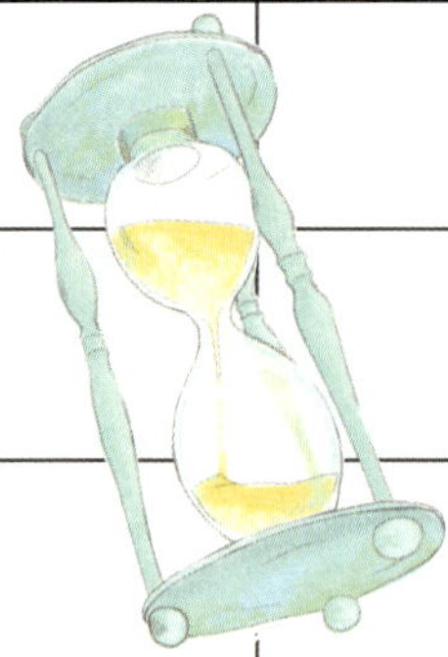

Adapted from *The Way Ahead*. Finch & Hyun (2000). Seoul: Hakmunsa. p. 24.

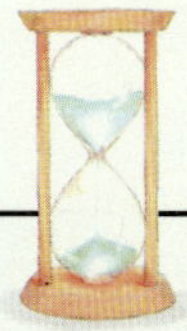

My Semester Planner

	Mon	Tues	Weds	Thurs	Fri	Sat	Sun
Week 1 月 日							
Week 2 月 日							
Week 3 月 日							
Week 4 月 日							
Week 5 月 日							
Week 6 月 日							
Week 7 月 日							
Week 8 月 日							
Week 9 月 日							
Week 10 月 日							
Week 11 月 日							
Week 12 月 日							
Week 13 月 日							
Week 14 月 日							
Week 15 月 日							

Adapted from *The Way Ahead*. Finch & Hyun (2000). Seoul: Hakmunsa. p. 25.

Ideas for the "My Reflections" pages

The 12 "My Reflections" pages in this journal (pages 11, 19, 26, etc.) are for your ideas. You can write about anything that is important to you on these pages, or you can write about the ideas that come up in class. If you can't think of anything to write about, here are some hints:

What do I think and feel about .....

* the English language? (difficult, easy, interesting)
* this course? (enjoyable, exciting, hard work)
* the learning environment? (see pages 47-50)
* my language ability? (see pages 20-32)
* my lifestyle? (see pages 56-57)
* my study routines? (see pages 28-29)
* my study skills? (see pages 40-42)
* my learning needs? (see pages 21-22)
* my goals and achievements? (see pages 24-25)
* my self-confidence? (see pages 55, 58)
* my motivation? (see page 43)
* my beliefs about learning? (see pages 34-38)
* my learning methods? (see pages 60-68)
* my learning style? (see pages 30-31)
* my multiple intelligences? (see pages 14-17)
* my problem-solving skills? (see pages 44, 67, 70, 71, 73)
* my study-planning? (see pages 52, 72, 84)

The goals of this journal include:

- thinking about learning;
- learning how to learn;
- interacting in English;
- improving writing skills.

In order to develop all these, we need to practice regularly. As the journal progresses, your ideas will grow in unexpected ways.

Let's begin — it's time to climb the mountain.

Personal profile

- **Ask someone** to interview you about your profile.
- **Ask him/her** to write your answers on this page.

Birthday:
Hometown:
Western Zodiac Sign:
Oriental Animal Sign:
Hobbies:
Best Friend:
Favorite Color:
Favorite Place:
Favorite Music:
Favorite Movie:
Favorite Sport:
Favorite TV Program:
Favorite Book:
Favorite Sportsperson:
Favorite Movie Actor/Actress:
Favorite Musician:
Favorite Korean Food:
Favorite Foreign Food:
My Likes:
My Hero/Heroine/Role model:
My Dream:
My Motto:

Education is for improving the lives of others and for leaving your community and world better than you found it. (Marian Wright Edelman)

Self-Assessment: What can we do now?

- **Talk with your classmates in groups of 4 or 5 people.**
- **Talk about your present level of English and fill in the grid below.**

5 = Yes, we can. (100%) **4** = Yes, mostly. (75%)
3 = Maybe. (50%) **2** = Not really. (25%) **1** = No, we can't. (0%)

Skills	***Questions***	***5***	***4***	***3***	***2***	***1***
Listening Skills: TV, radio, lectures, conversations	Can we understand movies in English?					
	Can we understand the TV News in English?					
	Can we understand Talk Shows in English?					
	Can we understand when the teacher talks in English?					
	Can we understand other students talking in English?					
	Can we understand lectures in English?					
Speaking Skills: conversations, interviews, travel, seminars, lectures, public speaking	Can we ask for information on the phone?					
	Can we ask for directions in English?					
	Can we ask questions abut personal information?					
	Can we ask about opinions in English?					
	Can we ask for permission to do something?					
	Can we talk about our lifestyles in English?					
	Can we talk about ourselves in English?					
	Can we introduce other people in English?					
	Can we hold a conversation in English?					
	Can we talk about our past experiences in English?					
	Can we talk about our opinions in English?					
	Can we make comments ("That's a good point," "It's funny you should say that," "On the other hand ..."etc.)?					
	Can we talk about current affairs in English?					
Presentations, Meetings: presenting, describing, discussing	Can we tell a story in English?					
	Can we tell a joke in English?					
	Can we talk about a movie for two minutes?					
	Can we talk about our majors in English?					
	Can we explain our ideas in English?					
	Can we debate in English?					
Writing Skills:	Can we write our resumés in English?					
	Can we write letters in English?					
	Can we write reports in English?					

Adapted from *The Way Ahead*. Finch & Hyun (2000). Seoul: Hakmunsa. p. 19.

Ideas that are important to me

- Exchange Books with your partner.
- Interview your partner.
- Write his/her answers on this page.

Q1. What ideas are important to you?

Q2. Which people are important to you? Why?

Q3. Who has influenced you? How?

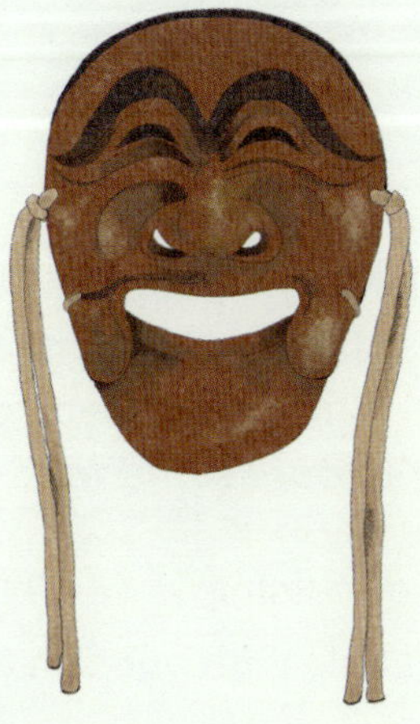

Learning is finding out what you already know. Doing is demonstrating that you know it. Teaching is reminding others that they know just as well as you. We are all learners, doers and teachers. (Richard Bach)

Star Signs

1. Ask everyone in the class:

- ▶ "When were you born?"
- ▶ "What star sign are you?"

Signs of the Zodiac		
♒ **Aquarius (water-carrier)** (Jan 21 - Feb 19) Name .... Name .... Name .... Name	♓ **Pisces (fish)** (Feb 20 - March 20) Name .... Name .... Name .... Name	♈ **Aries (ram)** (March 21 - April 20) Name .... Name .... Name .... Name ....
♉ **Taurus (bull)** (April 21 - May 21) Name .... Name .... Name .... Name	♊ **Gemini (twins)** (May 22 – June 21) Name .... Name .... Name .... Name	♋ **Cancer (crab)** (June 22 - July 22) Name .... Name .... Name .... Name ....
♌ **Leo (lion)** (July 23 - Aug 22) Name .... Name .... Name .... Name	♍ **Virgo (virgin)** (Aug 23 - Sept 23) Name .... Name .... Name .... Name	♎ **Libra (scales)** (Sept 24 - Oct 23) Name .... Name .... Name .... Name ....
♏ **Scorpio (scorpion)** (Oct 24 - Nov 22) Name .... Name .... Name .... Name	♐ **Sagittarius (archer)** (Nov 23 - Dec 22) Name .... Name .... Name .... Name	♑ **Capricorn (goat)** (Dec 23 - Jan 20) Name .... Name .... Name .... Name ....

2. FIND the people who have the SAME BIRTH SIGN AS YOU.

- Make a group, and talk about your Birth Sign.
- What sort of people are you (happy, patient, loving, organized, etc.)?
- Choose some words that describe YOU!

"People with our sign are..."

1. ....

2. ....

3. ....

4. ....

5. ....

My Reflections 1

- This is your first reflection page.
- Write about your personal details and your family.
- You can do this in your own time (at home).

My photo

Me

My family

Make a mind-map here to help you write your ideas.

My family's photo

(Title)

(Introduction)

(Body)

(Conclusion)

Autonomy and Self-Direction (1)

- How autonomous are you? Do you like studying by yourself?
- Exchange books and interview your partner.
- Read each question to your partner and circle (o) his/her 'Choice'.

Question 1	Answers	Choice
Why are you learning English?	... because I love learning languages.	Θ
	... because I want to learn about different cultures.	ℓ
	... in order to get a good job.	Δ
	... in order to pass an exam.	Φ
	... because I have no choice. English classes are compulsory.	Ω

Question 2	Answers	Choice
What is the best way to learn English?	... individual self-study without a teacher.	Θ
	... studying together in self-help groups.	ℓ
	... group studying in class with a teacher available.	Δ
	... individual studying in class with a teacher available.	Φ
	... listening to a teacher in class.	Ω

Question 3	Answers	Choice
What is the best study-speed for learning English?	... whatever I think is best for me.	Θ
	... whatever the students think is best for the group.	ℓ
	... whatever the students think is best for the class.	Δ
	... whatever the teacher thinks is best for me.	Φ
	... whatever the teacher thinks is best for the class.	Ω

Question 4	Answers	Choice
When is the best time to study English?	... whatever time I think is best for me.	Θ
	... whatever time the students think is best for the group.	ℓ
	... whatever time everyone thinks is best for the class.	Δ
	... whatever time the teacher thinks is best for me.	Φ
	... whatever time the teacher thinks is best for everyone.	Ω

Question 5	Answers	Choice
Where is the best place to study English? (home, classroom, library, computer room, etc.)	... whatever place I think is best for me.	Θ
	... whatever place the students think is best for the group.	ℓ
	... whatever place everyone thinks is best for the class.	Δ
	... whatever place the teacher thinks is best for me.	Φ
	... whatever place the teacher thinks is best for everyone.	Ω

Question 6	Answers	Choice
Who should choose what to study and how to study?	Everything should be chosen by me.	Θ
	Everything should be chosen by the groups.	ℓ
	Everything should be chosen by the groups and the teacher.	Δ
	The teacher should choose everything.	Φ
	The Ministry of Education should choose everything.	Ω

Autonomy and Self-Direction (2)

Question 7	Answers	Choice
How should our progress be monitored?	I should monitor my own progress.	ϴ
	Students should monitor each other (in groups).	ℓ
	The teacher should monitor my progress, when I ask him/her.	Δ
	The teacher should monitor the group's progress, when asked.	Φ
	The teacher should monitor everyone without being asked.	Ω

Question 8	Answers	Choice
How should learning be assessed (during the course)?	I should assess myself regularly.	ϴ
	The students (in groups) should assess themselves regularly.	ℓ
	The teacher should test me when I ask him/her.	Δ
	The teacher should give tests when everyone asks for them.	Φ
	The teacher should give tests without asking anyone.	Ω

Question 9	Answers	Choice
How should learning be assessed (independently of the course)?	I should be able to take an official exam (e.g. TEPS) if I want to.	ϴ
	Everyone should take an official exam if they want to.	ℓ
	I should choose which exam (e.g. IATEFL) to take.	Δ
	Everyone should have to take an exam. (e.g. TOEIC, TOEFL),	Φ
	The teacher should decide which exam students will take.	Ω

- Now add up the scores to find the Autonomy rating.

Score	Questions					
ϴ = 5 ℓ = 4 Δ = 3 Φ = 2 Ω = 1	1		2		3	
	4		5		6	
	7		8		9	
	Total /45					

'Autonomy' has at least five meanings. It can describe:

1. situations in which learners study entirely on their own;
2. skills which can be learned and used for self-directed learning;
3. a natural capacity for learning by oneself;
4. the exercise of learners' responsibility for their own learning;
5. the right of learners to decide what and how to learn.

How can we become more autonomous?

	Do I do this?	
• directed attention: concentrating on general aspects of a task;	Yes	No, not yet
• selective attention: paying attention to specific aspects of a task;	Yes	No, not yet
• self-monitoring: checking one's performance as one speaks;	Yes	No, not yet
• self-evaluation: assessing one's achievement of learning goals;	Yes	No, not yet
• self-reinforcement: rewarding oneself for success.	Yes	No, not yet

Adapted from Dickinson, L. (1986). Autonomy, self-directed learning and individualisation. In *ELT Documents 103 – Individualisation in Language Learning*: The British Council.

Multiple Intelligences Survey (MIS) (1)

We all have a mixture of different intelligences.

★ You can strengthen any of these intelligences.
★ Let's take a look at your Multiple Intelligences now.
★ You can learn more effectively by recognizing your MIs.

Instructions:

1. Exchange books with your partner.
2. Interview him/her about the statements in each section.
3. Write a "1" when he/she agrees with a statement.
4. Add the "1"s in each section, to make a total.

MI Survey, Section 1

_____ I enjoy classifying and putting things into categories.
_____ Ecological issues are important to me.
_____ Hiking and camping are enjoyable activities.
_____ I enjoy working on a garden (gardening).
_____ I believe that preserving our National Parks is important.
_____ Putting things in hierarchies (by importance) makes sense to me.
_____ Animals are important in my life.
_____ My home has a recycling system in place.
_____ I enjoy studying biology, botany and zoology.
_____ I spend a great deal of time outdoors.

TOTAL for Section 1 ____

MI Survey, Section 2

_____ I easily recognize patterns in pictures, music, carpets, etc.
_____ I am always aware of the noises and sounds around me.
_____ Moving to a musical beat is easy for me.
_____ I've always been interested in playing an instrument.
_____ The sound and rhythm of poetry intrigues me.
_____ I often remember things by putting them in a rhyme.
_____ Concentration is difficult while listening to the radio or television.
_____ I enjoy many kinds of music.
_____ Musicals are more interesting than dramatic plays.
_____ Remembering song lyrics is easy for me.

TOTAL for Section 2 ____

MI Survey, Section 3

_____ I keep my things neat and orderly.
_____ I like to follow step-by-step directions.
_____ Solving problems comes easily to me.
_____ I get easily frustrated with disorganized people.
_____ I can do calculations quickly in my head.
_____ Puzzles which need thinking and reasoning are fun.
_____ I can't begin an assignment until I know everything about it.
_____ Structuring my time helps me be successful.
_____ I find working on a computer spreadsheet or database rewarding.
_____ Things have to make sense to me or I am dissatisfied.

TOTAL for Section 3 ____

Multiple Intelligences Survey (2)

Section 4

_____ It is important to see my role in the 'big picture' of existence.
_____ I enjoy discussing questions about life.
_____ Religion is important to me.
_____ I enjoy viewing art masterpieces.
_____ Relaxation and meditation are rewarding activities.
_____ I like visiting breathtaking sites in nature.
_____ I enjoy reading ancient and modern philosophers.
_____ Learning new things is easier when I understand their value.
_____ I wonder if there are other forms of intelligent life in the universe.
_____ Studying history and ancient culture helps to give me perspective.

TOTAL for Section 4 ____

Section 5

_____ I learn best when interacting with others.
_____ I like working with people. The more, the merrier.
_____ Study groups are very productive for me.
_____ I enjoy chat rooms.
_____ Participating in politics is important.
_____ Television and radio talk shows are enjoyable.
_____ I am a team player.
_____ I dislike working alone.
_____ Clubs and extracurricular activities are fun.
_____ I pay attention to social issues and causes.

TOTAL for Section 5 ____

Section 6

_____ I enjoy making things with my hands.
_____ Sitting still for long periods of time is difficult for me.
_____ I enjoy outdoor games and sports.
_____ I value non-verbal communication such as sign language.
_____ A fit body is important for a fit mind.
_____ Arts and crafts are enjoyable pastimes.
_____ Expression through dance is beautiful.
_____ I like working with my hands and using tools.
_____ I live an active lifestyle.
_____ I learn by doing.

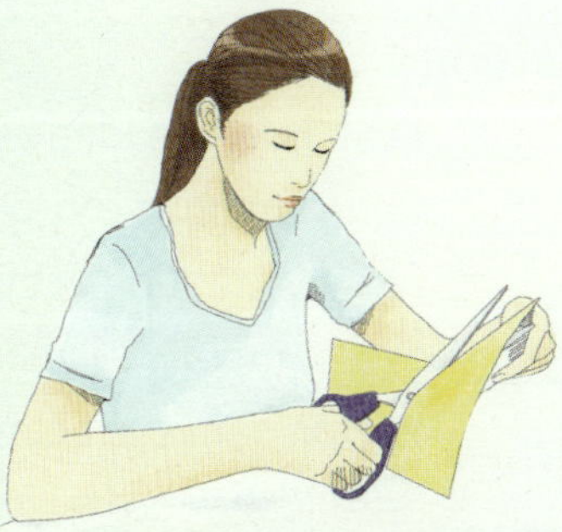

TOTAL for Section 6 ____

Multiple Intelligences Survey (3)

- Place a '1' next to each statement your partner agrees with.
- Then make a total for each section.

Section 7

_____ I enjoy reading all kinds of materials.
_____ Taking notes helps me remember and understand.
_____ I faithfully contact friends through letters and/or e-mail.
_____ It is easy for me to explain my ideas to others.
_____ I keep a diary.
_____ Word puzzles and crosswords are fun.
_____ I write for pleasure.
_____ I enjoy wordgames (puns, anagrams, double meanings, etc.).
_____ Foreign languages interest me.
_____ I like to participate in debates and public speaking activities.

TOTAL for Section 7 ____

Section 8

_____ I am keenly aware of my moral beliefs.
_____ I learn best when I have an emotional attachment to the subject.
_____ Fairness is important to me.
_____ My attitude affects how I learn.
_____ Social justice issues concern me.
_____ Working alone can be just as productive as working in a group.
_____ I need to know why I should do something before I agree to do it.
_____ When I believe in something I give 100% effort to it.
_____ I like to be involved in causes that help others.
_____ I am willing to protest or sign a petition to right a wrong.

TOTAL for Section 8 ____

Section 9

_____ I can imagine ideas in my mind.
_____ Rearranging a room is fun for me.
_____ I enjoy creating art using varied media.
_____ I remember well using graphic organizers.
_____ Performance art can be very gratifying.
_____ Spreadsheets are great for making charts, graphs and tables.
_____ Three dimensional puzzles bring me much enjoyment.
_____ Music videos are very stimulating.
_____ I can recall things in mental pictures.
_____ I am good at reading maps and blueprints.

TOTAL for Section 9 ____

Multiple Intelligences Survey (4)

Now plot your scores as a bar graph on this grid:

10									
9									
8									
7									
6									
5									
4									
3									
2									
1									
	Sec 1	Sec 2	Sec 3	Sec 4	Sec 5	Sec 6	Sec 7	Sec 8	Sec 9

Section 1 – This shows your Naturalist strength.
Section 2 – This shows your Musical strength.
Section 3 – This shows your Logical strength.
Section 4 – This shows your Existential strength.
Section 5 – This shows your Interpersonal strength.
Section 6 – This shows your Kinesthetic strength.
Section 7 – This shows your Verbal strength.
Section 8 – This shows your Intrapersonal strength.
Section 9 – This shows your Visual strength.

How is your MI profile?
What is your strongest intelligence type?
How about other members of the class?
What is your weakest intelligence type?
Is there anything you can do to improve it?
How does this survey help you in your studies?
Try this survey again some time in the future.

2-Minute Discussion

- **Everyone: Sit down** in two lines of chairs, facing each other.
- **Discuss** Topic 1 with the person opposite you for two minutes.
- **Stand up** and move to the chair on your left.
- **Discuss** Topic 2 with your new partner (2 minutes).
- **Stand up** and move to the chair on your left. (Continue)

Topic 1: Why are you taking this course?

Topic 2: How autonomous are you? (pages 12 - 13)

Topic 3: Tell me about your Multiple Intelligences. (page 17)

Topic 4: Who was your favorite teacher in high school? Why?

Topic 5: Were you a good student in school? Why? Why not?

Topic 6: What makes you happy in class? Why?

Topic 7: What makes you unhappy in class? Why?

Topic 8: What is learning? How do we learn?

Topic 9: What is the goal of education?

Topic 10: If you were Minister of Education … … … ?

My Reflections 2

- This is your journal (diary) page.
- You can write about anything here.
- Remember that your ideas and opinions are valid and important.
- Look at page 6 if you need some suggestions.

Date: ____________________

Title:

Let us think of education as the means of developing our greatest abilities, for the benefit of everyone and for the greater strength for our nation. (John F. Kennedy)

Education is not merely a means for earning a living. It is a training of the human soul in pursuit of truth and the practice of virtue. (Vijaya Lakshmi Pandit)

Who wants to …?

1. **Talk** to someone in the class.
2. **Ask** him/her one of the questions on this page.
3. **Talk** to a different person. **Ask** him/her one of the questions.
4. **ONE PERSON — ONE QUESTION!** How many boxes can you fill?

A) Excuse me. Do you want to understand movies in English? B) Yes, I do. A) What's your name? (Write the name.)	A) Excuse me. Do you want to study abroad? B) No, not really. A) O.K. Thank you anyway. (Don't write anything. Find another person.)

Do you want to understand movies in English? Name	Do you want to watch the news in English? Name	Do you want to express your ideas and opinions in English? Name ....
Do you want to read newspapers in English? Name	Do you want to tell stories in English? Name	Do you want to write a diary in English? Name ....
Do you want to write business letters in English? Name	Do you want to write emails in English? Name	Do you want to learn songs in English? Name ....
Do you want to talk with foreigners in English? Name	Do you want to guide tourists in English? Name	Do you want to understand lectures in English? Name ....
Do you want to give presentations in English? Name	Do you need to take interviews in English? Name	Do you want to read famous works of English literature? Name ....
Do you want to learn public speaking skills in English? Name	Do you want to explain about your major in English? Name	Do you want to use English language-learning websites? Name ....
Do you want to study abroad? Name	Do you want to work abroad? Name	Do you want to work for an international company in Korea? Name ....
Do you want to read academic journals in English? Name	Do you want to teach your child to speak in English? Name	Do you want to be a translator? Name ....
Do you want to teach English to elementary students? Name	Do you want to teach English in middle school? Name	Do you want to teach English in high school? Name ....

Self-Assessment "My learning"

Exchange books and interview your partner. Check (√) his/her responses.

"I need to think about my level of English now."

"How do you feel about your language learning skills?"	Poor	Ok	Great
My speaking skills in English are			
My listening skills in English are			
My reading skills in English are			
My writing skills in English are			
My communication skills in English are			
My pronunciation skills in English are			
My vocabulary skills (learning new words) are			
My study skills (autonomy, time-management) are			
My participation in class (effort, collaboration) is ...			
My confidence in learning English is ...			
My motivation for learning English is ...			
My attitude to learning English is			
My stress-management skills are ...			
My class attendance rate is ...			

"I need to think about when I use English."

"Do you ever...?"	Yes	Maybe	No
... speak in English in class?			
... ask for help from the teacher?			
... ask for help from other students?			
... study English at home?			
... watch TV programs in English?			
... watch movies in English?			
... read magazines in English?			
... read books in English?			
... talk to native speakers in English?			
... talk to friends in English?			
... talk to the teacher in his/her office?			
... send an email to the teacher?			

"I need to think about my learning needs."

"Do you need to learn English...?"	Yes	Maybe	No
... for studying your major?			
... for using the computer and the Internet?			
... for travel (business and pleasure)?			
... for your (future) job?			
... for talking to foreigners?			
... for studying abroad?			
... for passing an exam?			
... for other reasons?			

Adapted from *The Way Ahead*. Finch & Hyun (2000). Seoul: Hakmunsa. p. 16.

Students' Needs

- What do students need for learning a foreign language?
- Talk with the people in your group.
- Circle the number that matches the opinion of your group:
  1 = We agree strongly with this statement.
  2 = We agree with this statement on the whole.
  3 = We neither agree nor disagree with this statement.
  4 = We disagree with this statement on the whole.
  5 = We disagree strongly with this statement.

Students' personal and educational needs:	**Opinions**
Students need to be enthusiastic and passionate about learning.	1 2 3 4 5
Students need to have a positive attitude to learning.	1 2 3 4 5
Students need to be self-directed (autonomous).	1 2 3 4 5
Students need teachers who are good role models.	1 2 3 4 5
Students need to be treated fairly and equally by teachers.	1 2 3 4 5
Students need to be respected and trusted by teachers.	1 2 3 4 5
Students need teaching methods which treat them as individuals.	1 2 3 4 5
Students need teaching methods which suit their MIs (page 17).	1 2 3 4 5
Students need teaching methods which suit their Learning Styles (page 31).	1 2 3 4 5
Students need less emphasis on the textbook (more supplementary activities).	1 2 3 4 5
Students (S) need less TTT (teacher-talking-time) and more STT.	1 2 3 4 5
Students need a clear statement of the aims and content of a course.	1 2 3 4 5
Students need a variety of assessment methods (formative and summative).	1 2 3 4 5
Students need a comfortable learning environment.	1 2 3 4 5
Students need collaboration rather than competition.	1 2 3 4 5
Students need to learn study skills and learning strategies.	1 2 3 4 5
Students need help in dealing with stress and anxiety.	1 2 3 4 5
Students need help in managing emotions (anger, fear, depression, etc.).	1 2 3 4 5
Students need to learn how to assess themselves.	1 2 3 4 5
Students need to know about their progress.	1 2 3 4 5
Students need to know the results of all assessments.	1 2 3 4 5
Students need to see the relevance of subject content to their careers.	1 2 3 4 5
Students need to learn how to become good citizens.	1 2 3 4 5
Students need freedom to criticize their learning institution (school).	1 2 3 4 5
Students need to participate in educational decisions (syllabus, curriculum).	1 2 3 4 5

Based on Hills, P.J. (1976). *The Self-teaching Process in Higher Education*, Ch. 3. Student's and Teacher's Perceptions of Course Needs. Croom Helm: London.

Teachers' Needs

- What do teachers need for teaching a foreign language?
- Talk with your group members.
- Circle the number that matches the opinion of your group.
  1 = We agree strongly with this statement. 2 = We agree on the whole.
  3 = We neither agree nor disagree with this statement.
  4 = We disagree with this statement. 5 = We disagree strongly.
- How about making a survey of all the members in this class?

Teachers' personal and professional needs:	**Opinions**
Teachers need to be experts in their area (English, math, geography, history, etc).	1 2 3 4 5
Teachers need to develop a wide repertory of teaching skills.	1 2 3 4 5
Teachers need to keep up with new methods of teaching.	1 2 3 4 5
Teachers need to know about the psychology of learning.	1 2 3 4 5
Teachers need a strong philosophy of education.	1 2 3 4 5
Teachers need to be enthusiastic and energetic.	1 2 3 4 5
Teachers need to be organized and methodical.	1 2 3 4 5
Teachers need to enjoy teaching.	1 2 3 4 5
Teachers need time to prepare teaching materials.	1 2 3 4 5
Teachers need to reflect on their teaching.	1 2 3 4 5
Teachers need extra training opportunities (professional development).	1 2 3 4 5
Teachers need to be trusted and respected by students.	1 2 3 4 5
Teachers need feedback from students and other teachers.	1 2 3 4 5
Teachers need to listen to the wishes and opinions of parents.	1 2 3 4 5
Teachers need to know how effective their teaching is.	1 2 3 4 5
Teachers need to know how to assess students correctly.	1 2 3 4 5
Teachers need to make a non-threatening learning environment (classroom).	1 2 3 4 5
Teachers need teaching methods that suit different MIs (page 17) and LSs (page 31).	1 2 3 4 5
Teachers need to teach their students about learning strategies (page 64).	1 2 3 4 5
Teachers need to counsel their students, giving them advice and support.	1 2 3 4 5
Teachers need to give their students test-taking skills.	1 2 3 4 5
Teachers need to help students to be confident.	1 2 3 4 5
Teachers need to use logical arguments instead of authority.	1 2 3 4 5
Teachers need to stimulate intellectual curiosity in students.	1 2 3 4 5
Teachers need to do research.	1 2 3 4 5

Based on Hills, P.J. (1976). *The Self-teaching Process in Higher Education*, Ch. 3. Student's and Teacher's Perceptions of Course Needs. Croom Helm: London.

Learning Goals (1)

- Circle the items which are suitable for you.
- You can circle as many answers as you want.

1. What are my long term goals?

Become a teacher	Get married	Have a family	Start a business
Become rich	Help sick people	Speak many languages	Be an education official
Study abroad	Work abroad	Write a book	Other

2. What are my short term goals?

Be punctual	Exercise regularly	Get good grades	Graduate
Study regularly	Get a job	Learn computer skills	Help my parents
Live by myself	Make lots of friends	Earn money	Other

3. What do I need in order to achieve my goals?

Academic English	Business English	Diplomatic English
Medical English	Scientific English	Telephone English
Classroom English	Interview English	News English
Speed reading skills	Public speaking skills	Presentation skills
Communication skills	Writing skills	Business letter writing
Report writing	Resumé writing	Summary writing
Ability to listen to advice	Storytelling skills	Negotiation skills
Information accessing skills	Higher-order thinking skills	Computer skills
Networking skills	Logical reasoning skills	Self-esteem

4. What are my learning problems?

Computer skills	Examinations	Homework	Money (lack of)
Language level	Nervousness	Stress	Late for classes
Lack of confidence	Not enough sleep	Not enough study	Part-time job
Time management	Motivation (lack of)	Not asking for help	Other

5. How can I solve these problems?

When you have finished page 24, interview a classmate about his/her learning goals. (Exchange books.)

Learning Goals (2)

What are your long-term goals? • Which goal is most important to you? • Are you working on your goals now?	Notes
What are your short-term goals? • When do you want to achieve them? • Are you working on these goals now?	Notes
What do you need in order to achieve your long/short-term goals? • How can you satisfy these needs?	Notes
What learning problems do you have? • How can you solve them?	Notes
Do you plan your day? • Do you eat regularly? • Do you exercise regularly? • Do you balance study and free time?	Notes
Do you plan your study-time? • Do you miss homework deadlines? • Do you stay up late at night? • Do you get up late in the morning?	Notes
How can you plan your study time and free time more effectively?	Notes

You can find a week-planner and a semester-planner on pages 4 - 5.
How about using them to plan your time?

Adapted from *The Way Ahead*. Finch & Hyun (2000). Seoul: Hakmunsa, p. 21.

My Reflections 3

- This is your journal page.
- You can write about anything here.
- Check out page 6 for suggestions.

Date: ____________________

Title: ____

The only person who is educated is the one who has learned how to learn and change. (Carl Rogers)

Our Learning Preferences

- Groups of 3, 4, or 5 people.
- Discuss your study preferences.
- Put a different mark in the boxes for each person's opinion (# § Ø Δ θ etc.).

Our learning Preferences	No	Maybe	Yes
1. Extended reading is a good way to learn English.			
2. Listening activities are effective in learning English.			
3. Language games are an effective way to learn English.			
4. Speaking in class is a good way to learn English.			
5. Watching English-speaking movies is very helpful.			
6. Using a textbook is a good way to learn English.			
7. Listening to the teacher explain difficult grammar is very helpful.			
8. Teacher correction of our errors is very good for us.			
9. Groups and pairs are good for effective learning.			
10. Student-centered learning is very effective.			
11. Self-study outside of class is very effective.			
12. Watching English TV channels is a good way to learn English.			
13. Talking with native speakers is a good way to practice English.			
14. Writing on Internet blogs is a good way to practice English.			
15. Self-assessment is good for monitoring our achievements.			
16. Sending emails in English is a good way to practice English.			
17. Joining online chat rooms is a good way to practice English.			
18. Visiting English websites is good for learning English.			

- Here are 8 types of learning preferences. Where are you on these continua?
- Are you more Sensory than Intuitive? Are you more Verbal than Visual? Are you 50/50?
- Mark your position on the continua and discover your learning preference profile.

Sensory ←——————→		Intuitive
Sensory learners prefer practical and procedural information. They look for the facts.		Intuitive learners prefer ideas and theoretical information. They look for meaning.
Visual ←——————→		**Verbal**
Visual learners prefer graphs, pictures, and diagrams. They look for visual information.		Verbal learners prefer to hear or read information. They look for words.
Active ←——————→		**Reflective**
Active learners prefer to manipulate objects, do physical experiments, and learn by trying. They enjoy working in groups.		Reflective learners prefer to think, evaluate, and learn by analysis. They enjoy figuring out a problem on their own.
Sequential ←——————→		**Global**
Sequential learners prefer information presented in an orderly way. They put the details together in order to understand the big picture.		Global learners prefer a holistic and systematic approach. They see the big picture first and then fill in the details.

Study Habits: True or False?

Groups of 4 people.
Each person: Choose 3 statements (pages 28-29).

- Ask people in the class about your statements.
- Find out whether the statements are true or false.
- Report your findings to your group members.
- Summarize your group's findings on the next page.

How can you find out whether the statements are true or false? Do you have to ask everyone in the class?

1. Most people in this class study at home. **True/False**

2. Most people in this class like studying. **True/False**

3. Most people in this class study at night. **True/False**

4. Most people in this class study every day. **True/False**

5. Most people in this class listen to music while studying. **True/False**

6. Many people in this class study alone. **True/False**

7. Many people in this class study slowly and carefully. **True/False**

8. Many people in this class make notes when they study. **True/False**

9. Some people in this class remember things easily. **True/False**

10. Some people in this class write in the textbook when they study. **True/False**

11. Nobody in this class studies before breakfast. **True/False**

12. Nobody in this class watches TV when they study. **True/False**

Ask your group members for their results and write them here:

1 True/False	7 True/False
2 True/False	8 True/False
3 True/False	9 True/False
4 True/False	10 True/False
5 True/False	11 True/False
6 True/False	12 True/False

Adapted from *Now You're Talking!* Finch & Hyun (2000). Seoul: Hakmunsa, pp. 22-23.

Learning Style Inventory (1)

Different people have different learning styles.
If you know your style, you can learn more efficiently.

- Exchange books with your partner.
- Interview your partner: "Do you ... ?"
- What is your dominant learning style? Look at the following page to find out.

	My Learning Styles:	Yes, this is true of me.	This is sometimes true of me.	No, not really true of me.
1	I learn best through the teacher-led lecture method, with information, explanation, and discussion.			
2	I prefer information to be written on the board, along with visual aids and assigned readings.			
3	I write things down or take notes for visual review.			
4	I prefer to practice activities in class.			
5	I need explanations of diagrams, graphs, or visual directions.			
6	I enjoy working with my hands or making things.			
7	I am skillful at making graphs and charts.			
8	I can match (copy) sounds well (pronunciation).			
9	I remember things by writing them down many times.			
10	I can understand and follow directions on maps easily.			
11	I learn best by listening to lectures and audio recordings.			
12	I play with coins or keys in my pockets when studying.			
13	I learn to spell by repeating words, rather than writing them down.			
14	I understand a news article best by reading it (newspaper, Internet) rather than by listening to it on the radio.			
15	I chew gum, smoke, or eat snacks during my studies.			
16	I remember something best by picturing it in my head.			
17	I learn spelling by 'finger spelling' the words.			
18	I would rather listen to a good lecture than read about the same thing in a textbook.			
19	I am good at doing puzzles.			
20	I like to hold and touch things when I am learning.			
21	I prefer listening to the news on the radio rather than reading about it in a newspaper.			
22	I learn about a subject best by reading about it.			
23	I feel good about touching other people.			
24	I follow spoken directions better than written ones.			

Learning Style Inventory (2)

1. Look at your answers on page 30.
2. Write the scores for your answers in the table below:
    - Yes, this is true of me. = 5 points
    - This is sometimes true of me. = 3 points
    - No, not really true of me. = 1 point
3. Add the points to make a total.
4. 4. What type of learner are you? VPS? APS? TPS? 50/50?
5. Read the 'Hints' to find out your best learning strategies.

Visual	2		3		7		10		14		16		19		22		Total =
Auditory	1		5		8		11		13		18		21		24		Total =
Tactile	4		6		9		12		15		17		20		23		Total =

Hints for the Visual Preference Style (VPS) Learner:

- Take notes and make pictures, graphs or charts.
- Use flashcards and highlighters.
- Take notes or make lists as you listen to directions.
- Imagine pictures of the information you have to remember.
- Use color-coding for important information.
- Read and study in a well-lit, quiet place.
- Keep a note pad with you at all times.
- Write down everything for quick visual review.

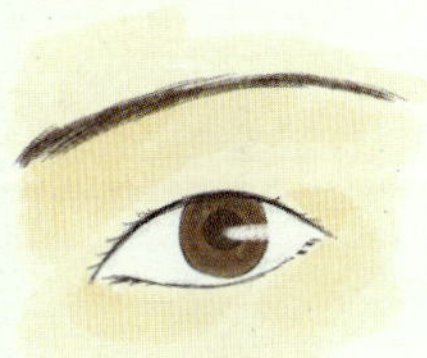

Hints for the Auditory Preference Style (APS) Learner:

- When you want to learn something, say it aloud, or record it and play it back to yourself.
- Read your work out loud.
- Summarize what you have read on tape or MP3 (voice recorder).
- Say words inside your head, silently.
- Brainstorm ideas with other people.
- Form study groups with other students.
- Learn information through CD-Roms, television, songs, radio, lectures, etc.
- Tape class lectures (voice recorder).

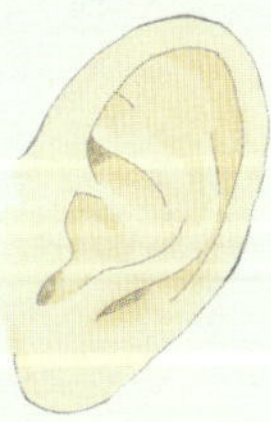

Hints for the Tactile Preference Style (TPS) learner:

- Keep your desk clear of distracting objects.
- Listen to soft music. Otherwise, turn off the radio.
- Work in short sessions. After 20 minutes or so, or when you finish a task, have a snack, walk around the block, listen to a song, etc.
- When possible, draw what you are learning.
- Write the shape of words are you practice them.
- Use models and real objects to help you learn.

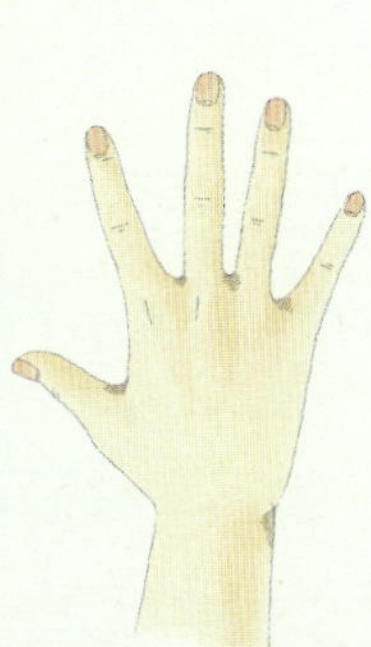

Adapted with permission from Martinez, M. (1997) Developing an intentional learning orientation questionnaire. Paper presented as a prospectus for a Measurement Project, IP & T 567R. Brigham Young University.

Group Discussion

- **Look** at the questions on this page.
- **Discuss** them together in your group.
- **WHILE** you are discussing, practice effective listening skills*.
    - **S**: Be **St**ill. Be **S**ilent
    - **H**: **H**ear what others are saying.
    - **A**: **A**llow others to speak and pay **A**ttention to them.
    - **R**: **R**estate what others say.
    - **E**: **E**ncourage others to speak.

1 Talk about your learning preferences (page 27).

2 Talk about your study habits (pages 28-29).

3 Talk about your learning styles (pages 30-31).

4 Talk about your Multiple Intelligences (page 17).

5 How can teachers take account of these factors (1-4) in the classroom?

6 Look at the 'Generational Learning' chart (below).**
- What does it show?
- Which generation are you?
- What relevance does this chart have for language teachers?
- How is English teaching changing with technology?

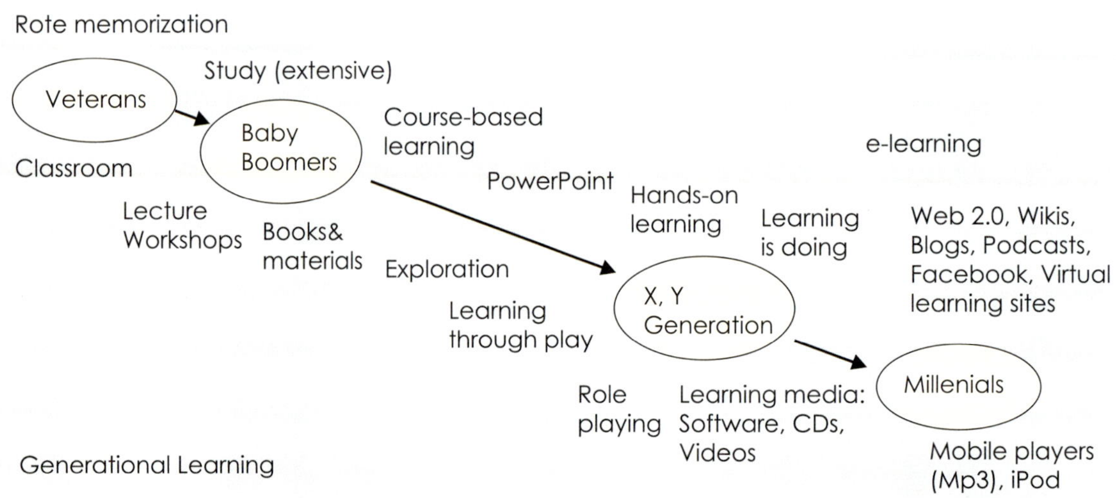

* "SHARE" effective listening skills adapted from *Educating the Heart*. Siccone & López (2000). pp. 191 – 194.
** Generational learning chart adapted from: http://nkilkenny.wordpress.com/

My Reflections 4

- This is your journal page.
- You can write about anything here.
- Check out page 6 for suggestions.

Date: ____________________

Title: ____

It seems that we learn lessons when we least expect them, but always when we need them the most, and the true "gift" in these lessons always lies in the learning process itself.
(Cathy Lee Crossby)

Beliefs About Language Learning

- We all have beliefs about learning a foreign language.
- Draw a circle around the number that matches your opinion:
  1 = I agree strongly.
  2 = I agree on the whole.
  3 = I neither agree nor disagree.
  4 = I disagree on the whole.
  5 = I disagree strongly.
- Talk to members of your group about your beliefs.

	Students' personal and educational needs:	**Opinions**
1	When learning a language, structure and vocabulary are most important.	1 2 3 4 5
2	Speaking the new language is more important than learning grammar.	1 2 3 4 5
3	Some languages are easier to learn than others.	1 2 3 4 5
4	Learning a language is different to learning other subjects.	1 2 3 4 5
5	Some people have a special ability to learn languages.	1 2 3 4 5
6	Women are better than men at learning a new language.	1 2 3 4 5
7	Children learn a new language easier than adults.	1 2 3 4 5
8	Language teachers should always be learning a new language.	1 2 3 4 5
9	The role of the teacher is to help students prepare for examinations.	1 2 3 4 5
10	The role of the teacher is to help students learn how to learn.	1 2 3 4 5
11	The role of the teacher is to stimulate curiosity.	1 2 3 4 5
12	The role of the teacher is to prepare students for adult life.	1 2 3 4 5
13	Learning a new language improves the character of the student.	1 2 3 4 5
14	Learning a new language develops cultural awareness.	1 2 3 4 5
15	Everyone has the ability to learn a foreign language.	1 2 3 4 5
16	It is best to learn English in an English-speaking country.	1 2 3 4 5
17	It is most important to think in the new language.	1 2 3 4 5
18	Beginners should always be corrected.	1 2 3 4 5
19	Studying for an hour a day is enough to learn a language fluently.	1 2 3 4 5
20	It is necessary to know the culture in order to speak a language well.	1 2 3 4 5
21	If I can speak a foreign language, it will be easy to learn another one.	1 2 3 4 5
22	It is not always best to have language teachers who are native-speakers.	1 2 3 4 5
23	Languages are best learned in an immersion situation.	1 2 3 4 5
24	Everyone should learn to speak at least one foreign language.	1 2 3 4 5

Loosely based on the *Beliefs And Language Learning Inventory* (BALLI) of Horwitz, 1988.

My Perceptions About Language Learning

How do I learn best? What is the best method of learning for me?

1. Check (√) the box that matches your opinion.
    - No = I don't agree. This is not good for me.
    - So-so = This is neither good nor bad for me.
    - Yes = I agree on the whole. This learning method is good for me.
    - Great = I totally agree. This learning method is great for me.
2. Discuss your perceptions with your group members.
3. Use different signs for their opinions: e.g. ☺ ♀ ♂ ±

	Students' personal and educational needs:	No	So-so	Yes	Great
1	In English class, we learn best by reading.				
2	In English class, we learn best by listening.				
3	In English class, we learn best by playing games.				
4	In English class, we learn best by having conversations.				
5	In English class, we learn best by watching videos.				
6	I learn best by making notes in my notebook.				
7	I learn best by using a textbook.				
8	I learn best when the teacher gives us grammar problems.				
9	I learn best when the teacher tells me my mistakes.				
10	I learn best by correcting myself.				
11	I learn best when studying by myself.				
12	I learn best when studying in groups in class.				
13	I learn best by watching TV and movies in English.				
14	If we don't understand, it is best to ask someone to explain.				
15	It is helpful to watch people's faces and hands when they are talking. This gives us non-verbal clues about meaning.				
16	It is best to try to use English, even if we make mistakes.				
17	We should try to find ways to use English outside of class.				
18	We should think about what we will say, before we speak.				
19	We should listen to ourselves when we speak.				
20	When we learn a word, we should use it in conversation.				
21	If someone does not understand us, we should try to say the same thing in a different way.				
22	We should try to find our problems and fix them.				
23	We should always look for better ways to learn.				

Adapted from Willing, K. (1988). *Learning Styles in Adult Migrant Education*, pp. 106-7, Adelaide, Australia: National Curriculum Resource Centre.

Stereotypes 1

Groups of 4: Two people (1, 2) look at this page. Two people (3, 4) look at page 37.

Two people (1, 2): Below are descriptions of five people.

- **Talk** together about the information given.
- **Circle** the numbers which indicate what sort of person each one is.
- **Make** a total score for each person.
- **Discuss** the results with the other pair (3, 4).
- **Talk** about stereotypes and the effect that stereotyping has on people.
- **Discuss** what relevance this activity has for English teachers.

Hee-su is 21 years old and a senior in college. She is 160 cm tall and meets her boyfriend about twice a week. She likes wearing fancy clothes and perfume. She is probably :						
Intelligent	5	4	3	2	1	Stupid
Easygoing	5	4	3	2	1	Hot-tempered
Liberal	5	4	3	2	1	Conservative
Attractive	5	4	3	2	1	Unattractive
	Total =					

Frank is 32, black, married to a high school graduate, and works for IBM Korea. He is probably:						
Friendly	5	4	3	2	1	Unfriendly
Intelligent	5	4	3	2	1	Stupid
Good public speaker	5	4	3	2	1	Poor public speaker
Steady	5	4	3	2	1	Temperamental
Ambitious	5	4	3	2	1	Lazy
	Total =					

Mohammed is 34. He works in a textile factory in Daegu and sends money to his wife and six children in Manila. He is probably:						
Friendly	5	4	3	2	1	Unfriendly
Intelligent	5	4	3	2	1	Stupid
Ambitious	5	4	3	2	1	Lazy
Happy-go-lucky	5	4	3	2	1	Serious
	Total =					

Da-bin works at Samsung Phone Company, is married, and has one child. She is probably:						
Competent	5	4	3	2	1	Incompetent
Content	5	4	3	2	1	Discontent
Rational	5	4	3	2	1	Emotional
Artistic	5	4	3	2	1	Scientific
	Total =					

Hyun-min is a 27-year-old medical student. He travels in the summer, dates most weekends, and likes cars. He is probably:						
Intelligent	5	4	3	2	1	Stupid
Polite	5	4	3	2	1	Rude
Law-abiding	5	4	3	2	1	Law-breaker
Nice guy	5	4	3	2	1	Bad guy
	Total =					

Stereotypes 2

Groups of 4: Two people (3, 4) look at this page. Two people (1, 2) look at page 36.

Two people (3, 4): Below are descriptions of five people.

- **Talk** together about the information given.
- **Circle** the numbers which best indicate what sort of person each one is.
- **Make** a total score for each person.
- **Discuss** the results with the other pair (1, 2).
- **Talk** about stereotypes and the effect that stereotyping has on people.
- **Discuss** what relevance this activity has for English teachers.

Min-su is 21 years old and a senior in college. He is 160 cm tall and meets his boyfriend about twice a week. He likes wearing fancy clothes and perfume. He is probably :						
Intelligent	5	4	3	2	1	Stupid
Easygoing	5	4	3	2	1	Hot-tempered
Liberal	5	4	3	2	1	Conservative
Attractive	5	4	3	2	1	Unattractive
	Total =					

Frank is 32, black, married to a (Korean) high school graduate, and is a colonel in the American Forces Korea. He is probably:						
Friendly	5	4	3	2	1	Unfriendly
Intelligent	5	4	3	2	1	Stupid
Good public speaker	5	4	3	2	1	Poor public speaker
Steady	5	4	3	2	1	Temperamental
Ambitious	5	4	3	2	1	Lazy
	Total =					

Mohammed is 34. He works in a textile factory in Daegu and sends money to his wife and six children in Pakistan. He is probably:						
Friendly	5	4	3	2	1	Unfriendly
Intelligent	5	4	3	2	1	Stupid
Ambitious	5	4	3	2	1	Lazy
Happy-go-lucky	5	4	3	2	1	Serious
	Total =					

Mr. Kim works at Samsung Phone Company, is married, and has one child. He is probably:						
Competent	5	4	3	2	1	Incompetent
Content	5	4	3	2	1	Discontent
Rational	5	4	3	2	1	Emotional
Artistic	5	4	3	2	1	Scientific
	Total =					

Hyun-min is a 27-year-old middle-school teacher. He travels in the summer, dates most weekends, and likes cars. He is probably:						
Intelligent	5	4	3	2	1	Stupid
Polite	5	4	3	2	1	Rude
Law-abiding	5	4	3	2	1	Law-breaker
Nice guy	5	4	3	2	1	Bad guy
	Total =					

Discussion: Language Learning Ideas

Here are some ideas about language learning.

- **Draw** a cross (X) at the point on each continuum that matches your opinion.
- **Discuss** the ideas with people in your group.
- **Make** a mark (e.g. Θ) at the points that match your group's opinion.
- **Change groups** - discuss with the new group.

Ideas, beliefs and perceptions about learning:

Beliefs and perceptions control learning. Affective filters can prevent learning.

I/we agree with this statement. ⟷ I/we disagree with this statement.

Motivation is more important than ability in learning a language.

I/we agree with this statement. ⟷ I/we disagree with this statement.

Students do not learn what the teacher teaches. They learn what they want to learn.

I/we agree with this statement. ⟷ I/we disagree with this statement.

Language learning is not linear. It is cyclic, repetitive and formative.

I/we agree with this statement. ⟷ I/we disagree with this statement.

A language is more than the sum of its parts. It is acquired in an integrated manner.

I/we agree with this statement. ⟷ I/we disagree with this statement.

Collaboration is more effective than competition in language learning.

I/we agree with this statement. ⟷ I/we disagree with this statement.

Students need to learn higher-order thinking skills rather than test-preparation skills.

I/we agree with this statement. ⟷ I/we disagree with this statement.

Language teaching should focus on education and development of the whole person.

I/we agree with this statement. ⟷ I/we disagree with this statement.

Students work hardest on activities that are assessed and graded.

I/we agree with this statement. ⟷ I/we disagree with this statement.

English is a lingua franca of this global world we live in. We cannot do without it.

I/we agree with this statement. ⟷ I/we disagree with this statement.

It is important to speak English like a native speaker.

I/we agree with this statement. ⟷ I/we disagree with this statement.

Going abroad to learn English is an extremely valuable experience.

I/we agree with this statement. ⟷ I/we disagree with this statement.

Adapted from Hahn, S.L. (1989). Grading classroom activities: Effects on motivation and proficiency. *Foreign Language Annals*, 22, No. 3.

My Reflections 5

- This is your journal page.
- You can write about anything here.
- Check out page 6 for suggestions.

Date: ____________________

Title: ____________________

The secret in education lies in respecting the student.
(Ralph Waldo Emerson)

Study Skills: Memory (1)

This is a loop activity. Its content is about its learning goal.

- Try to solve these paragraphs, and see if they help your memory.
- Use the next page to write out the correct versions.
- Can you find a suitable order for the paragraphs? (1, 2, 3, ...)

one caused by personal factors and the other by a poor environment for study. Personal or course-related anxiety, The major cause of poor concentration is studying while you are distracted. daydreaming and lack of rest are the most common barriers to successful concentration. Two types of distraction are common,

Your memory _ _ _ be improved. Human memory _ _ _ been studied and found _ _ have certain patterns. For example, _ _ tend _ _ remember things which we _ _ _ _ heard first, or most recently. You shouldn't study _ _ _ long stretches _ _ time, _ _ _ _ _ _ _ _ you will forget most of what _ _ _ study _ _ that time. It is better _ _ break your studying _ _ _ _ small periods _ _ time, so that you have less _ _ _ _ in-between to forget things.

Memory is also enhanced by making associations between your notes, and organizing and summarizing your notes into essential ideas, perhaps in the form of a diagram. Finally, constant recitation and review of course material will improve your ability to remember what you studied.

and which is a place where you will only study to maximize your concentration. are the wrong places to study. poorly lit or ventilated, You should pick a study spot which doesn't strain your eyes or body, or where you normally do other things, where all the supplies you need are on hand, Places which are noisy,

Two frequent complaints of students are that they can't concentrate while studying, and that they can't remember the material which they studied. There are many techniques for improving your concentration and memory, although you will have to see which one suits you best.

of One key the for elements concentration successful to is what plan are you to going in study of order priority. you If a spend of lot reviewing time which information not is vital, will you trouble have concentrating. should You break also study your up time manageable into of periods time, schedule and regular a break.

Study Skills: Memory (2)

The major cause of

1 Your memory can be

Memory is also enhanced by

Places which are noisy,

Two frequent complaints

One of the key elements

Study Skills Interview:

- Talk to a classmate about study skills, using the questions below.
- Ask "Why?", especially when you get an interesting answer.

Question		Answer
1	Do the things you have learnt reflect the amount of time you spend studying?	
2	Do you usually cram all night before an exam?	
3	If you spent as much time on social activities as you wanted to, would this harm your studies?	
4	Do you study with the radio, CD, or TV turned on?	
5	Can you study for long periods of time without becoming tired or distracted?	
6	When you go to class, do you usually doodle, daydream, or fall asleep?	
7	Are your class notes sometimes difficult to understand when you look at them later?	
8	Do you review your class notes regularly during the semester in preparation for tests?	
9	When you get to the end of a chapter in a textbook, can you remember everything?	
10	Do you know how to find the main point in study texts and other books?	
11	Do you ever browse the Internet for Study Skills sites and language learning sites?	
12	Do you lose points on written tests even when you know the material well?	
13	Has your mind ever gone blank in an exam, even though you had studied well for the test?	
14	Do you study in a random, disorganized way when preparing for the next test?	
15	Do you get lost in the minor details when reading, and then have trouble identifying the main ideas?	
16	Do you make notes while reading a textbook?	
17	Do you ever wish that you could read faster?	
18	When the teacher sets assignments, do you ever feel so overwhelmed that you can't get started?	
19	Do you ever spend too much time on one question when you take a test?	
20	Do you have problems organizing your thoughts when you write assignments?	

The dynamic triangle of motivation

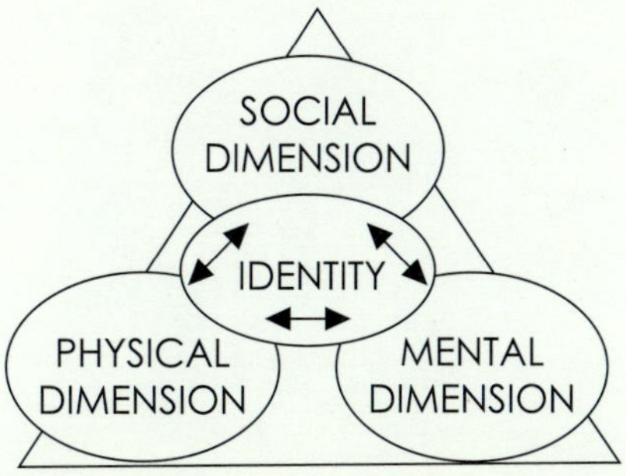

Self–Assessment: Motivation

Motivation in learning is very important:
- It encourages us to make goals and achieve them.
- It promotes confidence and positive attitudes.
- It encourages us to concentrate and understand language.
- It encourages us to interact and communicate with others.
- It gives us a passion for learning.

My Motivation Profile:

	True .... not true
1. I want to learn English.	⟷
2. I need to learn English to get a good job.	⟷
3. I want to improve my language-learning strategies.	⟷
4. I want to make my own goals and plan my learning.	⟷
5. I want to assess my achievements.	⟷
6. I want to develop my higher-order thinking skills.	⟷
7. I will continue to study. Effort is the mother of success	⟷
8. I always look for effective methods of learning.	⟷
9. I want to understand everything in class.	⟷
10. I participate in class even if I am embarrassed or nervous.	⟷
11. I always ask the teacher for help when I need it.	⟷
12. If I have a problem, I always try to find the solution.	⟷
13. Whatever the situation, I always do my best.	⟷
14. I always try to overcome my anxiety and nervousness.	⟷
15. Making mistakes is part of learning.	⟷
16. I take risks when speaking English. This is the best way to improve.	⟷
17. I don't need to be threatened or punished to make me learn.	⟷
18. I don't need points or rewards to make me learn.	⟷
19. I enjoy learning for its own sake. I will always learn.	⟷
20. I am always thinking (reflecting) about my learning.	⟷

1. Take some time to think about your learning:
   - *Why am I learning English?*
   - *What are my learning needs?*
   - *What do I want to achieve?*
   - *How can I learn most effectively?*
2. Look at Maslow's Needs Pyramid (right).
   - *What are your needs?*
   - *Where are you in this pyramid?*
   - *How can motivation help you?*

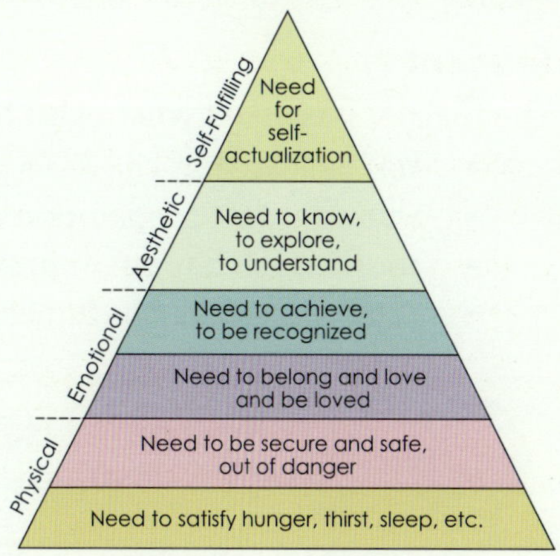

Learner-Counseling: Role Play

Four people: Try this role play.

- Use these prompts as hints and starting points.
- Have some deep discussion between teacher and students.
- Use your imagination - be creative!

Teacher

You have asked some students to come to your office to discuss their learning problems:

- Student a) is anxious and lacks confidence about his/her abilities.
- Student b) is not motivated to do any study (poor attitude).
- Student c) has no initiative, and is a very passive learner (poor at participation).

Student a)

The teacher has asked you to visit his/her office to discuss your learning problem.

- You believe that you are a poor learner.
- You don't think you will ever be able to learn English.
- You hope there won't be many other students in the office.
- You feel very nervous.

Student b)

The teacher has asked you to visit his/her office to discuss your learning problem.

- You don't want to talk with the teacher.
- You don't like studying English. It's very boring.
- You don't need English for your future.
- In your opinion, this is a waste of time.

Student c)

The teacher has asked you to visit his/her office to discuss your learning problem.

- You believe that you are a good student, though you never participate in class.
- You want test-preparation, not communication or interaction.
- Your English has not improved this semester.
- You have too much studying to do in other subjects.

Well done! How about making a video of your role play?
How about making a different role play?

My Reflections 6

- This is your journal page.
- You can write about anything here.
- Check out page 6 for suggestions.

Date: ____________________

Title:

The principal goal of education is to create men who are capable of doing new things, not simply of repeating what other generations have done - men who are creative, inventive and discoverers. (Jean Piaget)

Peer Feedback

- We are half way through the journal.
- Well done for all your efforts so far!
- Now give your journal to a classmate.
- Your classmate will give you written feedback about your journal.
- Later on, the teacher will give you written feedback as well.

Date: ____________________

Title:

You can no more learn a language without making mistakes than you can learn to play tennis without ever hitting the ball into the net. (H. Douglas Brown)

Classroom Learning Environment

* How is our classroom? Does it help us to learn?
* How are the lessons? Do they encourage us to learn?
* How is the teacher? Does he/she motivate us to learn?
* Let's think about our learning environment.
* Is it collaborative/competitive, stressful/comfortable?
* Y = Yes; M = Maybe; N = No;

Our learning environment ...	**Y**	**M**	**N**
1. ... encourages us to be active.			
2. ... encourages us to discover our own ideas.			
3. ... emphasizes the personal nature of learning.			
4. ... encourages differences as good and desirable.			
5. ... recognizes our right to make mistakes.			
6. ... tolerates ambiguity (allows for contradictions).			
7. ... views evaluation as cooperative and personal.			
8. ... encourages openness of self.			
9. ... encourages us to trust ourselves.			
10. ... is one in which we feel respected.			
11. ... is one in which we feel accepted.			
12. ... permits confrontation, negotiation and reconciliation.			
13. ... allows the teacher to lose the teaching function.			
14. ... attempts to meet individual needs and abilities.			
15. ... provides meaningful learning materials.			
16. ... promotes personal interests and exploration.			
17. ... provides materials that need interaction.			
18. ... promotes collaboration over competition.			
19. ... allows us to make mistakes and still feel OK.			
20. ... helps us grow socially, emotionally, and intellectually.			
21. ... nurtures respect and trust for one another.			
22. ... views the teacher's role as facilitator.			

Based on Pine, G.J. & Boy, A.V. (1977). *Learner Centered Teaching: A Humanistic View*. Denver: Love Publishing.

Classroom Environment Questionnaire (Preferred)

Group-work: Circle the numbers that match the opinion of your group.

1= We would be happy if this never happened in class.
2= We would be happy if this rarely happened in class.
3= We would be happy if this sometimes happened in class.
4= We would be happy if this often happened in class.
5= We would be happy if this always happened in class.

1	Students come to class early and prepare for the lesson.	**1 2 3 4 5**
2	Students talk in English before the teacher arrives.	**1 2 3 4 5**
3	The teacher comes to class early and starts the lesson on time.	**1 2 3 4 5**
4	The teacher decides which students work together.	**1 2 3 4 5**
5	The teacher explains grammar at the students' request.	**1 2 3 4 5**
6	Students choose which tasks (projects) to do.	**1 2 3 4 5**
7	The teacher explains how to do tasks at the students' request.	**1 2 3 4 5**
8	Students work at their own speed when performing the tasks.	**1 2 3 4 5**
9	Learning is project-based and student-centered.	**1 2 3 4 5**
10	There are no prizes or punishments for classwork.	**1 2 3 4 5**
11	Students are responsible for much of the assessment.	**1 2 3 4 5**
12	The teacher facilitates learning rather than controlling it.	**1 2 3 4 5**
13	Students talk in the target language at all times.	**1 2 3 4 5**
14	The teacher occasionally gives a lecture, when necessary.	**1 2 3 4 5**
15	The teacher helps students individually.	**1 2 3 4 5**
16	Students give presentations about their projects.	**1 2 3 4 5**
17	The learning environment is conducive to stress-free learning.	**1 2 3 4 5**
18	Assessment is ongoing and formative.	**1 2 3 4 5**
19	Collaboration is encouraged instead of competition.	**1 2 3 4 5**
20	Students develop cognitive, affective, social and linguistic skills.	**1 2 3 4 5**

Adapted from Fraser, B. J. (1986). *Classroom Environment*. London: Croom Helm.

Classroom Environment Questionnaire (Actual)

Group-work: Circle the numbers that match the opinion of your group.
1= This never happens in class.
2= This rarely happens in class.
3= This sometimes happens in class.
4= This often happens in class.
5= This always happens in class.

1	Students come to class early and prepare for the lesson.	1 2 3 4 5
2	Students talk in English before the teacher arrives.	1 2 3 4 5
3	The teacher comes to class early and starts the lesson on time.	1 2 3 4 5
4	The teacher decides which students work together.	1 2 3 4 5
5	The teacher explains grammar at the students' request.	1 2 3 4 5
6	Students choose which tasks (projects) to do.	1 2 3 4 5
7	The teacher explains how to do tasks at the students' request.	1 2 3 4 5
8	Students work at their own speed when performing the tasks.	1 2 3 4 5
9	Learning is project-based and student-centered.	1 2 3 4 5
10	There are no prizes or punishments for classwork.	1 2 3 4 5
11	Students are responsible for much of the assessment.	1 2 3 4 5
12	The teacher facilitates learning rather than controlling it.	1 2 3 4 5
13	Students talk in the target language at all times.	1 2 3 4 5
14	The teacher occasionally gives a lecture, when necessary.	1 2 3 4 5
15	The teacher helps students individually.	1 2 3 4 5
16	Students give presentations about their projects.	1 2 3 4 5
17	The learning environment is conducive to stress-free learning.	1 2 3 4 5
18	Assessment is ongoing and formative.	1 2 3 4 5
19	Collaboration is encouraged instead of competition.	1 2 3 4 5
20	Students develop cognitive, affective, social and linguistic skills.	1 2 3 4 5

- Now compare your results with page 48.
- How does the preferred learning environment (page 48) differ from the actual learning environment (page 49)?
- How significant are these results?
- What should the teacher do about the preferred/actual differences?

Adapted from Fraser, B. J. (1986). *Classroom Environment*. London: Croom Helm.

Classroom Environment Scale (CES)

Think about your middle school or high school times.
Did you enjoy studying? Who was your best teacher?

- **Talk** about the best classes in your secondary schools.
- How was the classroom environment?
- Add your own comments for 19 and 20 (below).

y = "Yes. This is true."
m = "Maybe yes, maybe no."
n = "No. This is not true."

The (best) learning environment in secondary school				
1	The classes were well prepared and well organized.	y	m	n
2	The teacher was a good role model for the students.	y	m	n
3	This classes were student-centered.	y	m	n
4	Classroom-based assessment was used (portfolios, self-assessment, peer-assessment, presentations, etc.).	y	m	n
5	Students put a lot of energy into the class and worked very hard.	y	m	n
6	Students got to know each other well in this class.	y	m	n
7	Students often talked about this class when it was over.	y	m	n
8	Students daydreamed in this class and even went to sleep.	y	m	n
9	Students helped each other to keep the classroom clean.	y	m	n
10	Students always wanted to leave early.	y	m	n
11	Students listened closely to the teacher.	y	m	n
12	Students did a lot of study outside of class.	y	m	n
13	The teacher took a personal interest in every student.	y	m	n
14	The teacher was a monitor and facilitator of learning.	y	m	n
15	The teacher tried to help all the students.	y	m	n
16	Many friendships were made in this classroom.	y	m	n
17	The classroom was often noisy.	y	m	n
18	The atmosphere in the classroom was friendly and non-threatening.	y	m	n
19		y	m	n
20		y	m	n

Adapted from Fraser, B. J. (1986). *Classroom Environment*. London: Croom Helm.

Self–Assessment: Participation

Participation in learning is very important:

- It helps us to focus on learning content and meaning.
- It helps us to concentrate and understand.
- It encourages us to interact and communicate with others.
- It promotes confidence, motivation and positive attitudes.

My Class-Participation Profile: 5 = Always; 4 = Usually; 3 = Sometimes 2 = Occasionally; 1 = Rarely; 0 = Never	
1. I prepare for class by reading about the lesson content.	
2. I come to class early, so that I am ready to start on time.	
3. I speak in English whenever I can.	
4. I listen carefully to my group members.	
5. I offer creative ideas to my group.	
6. I participate in all the activities.	
7. I ask the teacher for help when necessary.	
8. Whatever the situation, I do my best.	
9. I try to develop critical thinking and problem-solving strategies.	
10. I think about the class ("What am I learning?").	
11. I think about my learning ("How am I doing?").	
12. I do the homework and out-of-class assignments.	
13. I review the lesson to reinforce my learning.	
My Self-Study-Participation Profile:	
14. I keep a diary in English.	
15. I watch English-speaking videos and TV programs.	
16. I ask the teacher for advice on what and how to learn.	
17. I talk in English with friends.	
18. I write emails in English to my friends.	
19. I look for language-learning websites.	
20. I talk to myself in English.	
Total	

1. Write the numbers that describe your participation.
2. Add the numbers to make a total. What is your %?
3. Take some time to think about your participation:
   - What do I want to achieve?
   - How can I learn most effectively?
   - Am I doing enough?

The Pre-Nuptial Agreement

- We will make 3 contracts in this book.
- They will help us think about responsibility and social skills.
- First, let's think about (interpersonal) responsibility between a couple.
- What are the most important things in a relationship?
- Is love enough? Is money enough? How about children?

This is a contract between .... and ....
These are the conditions for our marriage.
If either person breaks these conditions, the marriage will be over.

1. We must ______
2. We must ______
3. We must ______
4. We must not ______
5. We must not ______
6. We must not ______
7. We should ______
8. We should ______
9. We should not ______
10. We should not ______

Signatures ______

______

Witness ______

Date ______

Adapted from Fraser, B. J. (1986). *Classroom Environment*. London: Croom Helm.

My Reflections 7

- This is your journal page.
- You can write about anything here.
- Check out page 6 for suggestions.

Date: ____________________

Title:

Learning isn't a means to an end; it is an end in itself.
(Robert Heinlein)

A Good Thing: Groups

Purpose: Three stress reduction techniques are looked at in this activity: 1, Relaxation; 2, "Stop thought"; and 3, Transformation of negative messages into positive ones. These techniques can reduce or eliminate stress before it affects language learning.

1. Speaker:
Read this text very slowly:

Everybody except the speaker: Keep your eyes closed. Listen and follow the instructions for 1, 2 and 3.

Quiet.
Only quiet.
Let's be quiet.
Breathe in.
Breathe out.
Close your eyes.
Listen to the person reading the text.

2. Speaker:
Read this text very slowly:

"STOP THOUGHT"

When negative thoughts begin, imagine a STOP sign, or say "stop!" to yourself. Then take some deep breaths from your stomach.

Hold your breath for a moment or two and exhale slowly, softly and steadily.

At the same time, tell your body to go limp or melt.

3. Speaker:
Read this text very slowly:

- Think of negative thoughts, such as "I'm going to fail the test."
- Now change the negative thoughts into positive ones.
- Say to yourself "I will pass the test."
- Instead of saying "I am a poor at speaking the target language," say "My fluency is improving all the time."
- Think of some more negative thoughts.
- Use **stop-thought** and **deep-breathing** and then transform them into positive ones.

EVERYBODY: Now think of something GOOD that happened to you today.
Tell everyone about it.
Let's share our thoughts.

Adapted from *The Way Ahead*. Finch & Hyun (2000) p. 162 and *Educating the Heart*. Siccone & López (2000) p. 42.

Foreign Language Classroom Anxiety Scale (FLCAS)

- Do you get nervous in the foreign language class?
- Do you get anxious and worried?
- Is the foreign language class stressful?
- Have a look at this questionnaire to find out your Anxiety rating.
- Circle the numbers that match your situation.

1 = I strongly agree.
2 = I agree on the whole.
3 = I neither agree nor disagree.
4 = I disagree on the whole.
5 = I strongly disagree.

1	I get nervous when the teacher speaks to me.	**1 2 3 4 5**
2	I am embarrassed when I answer the teacher.	**1 2 3 4 5**
3	I worry about making mistakes in English class.	**1 2 3 4 5**
4	I get nervous when speaking in English in class.	**1 2 3 4 5**
5	My heart pounds when I have to do something in class.	**1 2 3 4 5**
6	I feel self-conscious when speaking in English with my classmates.	**1 2 3 4 5**
7	I am afraid that others will laugh at me when I speak in English.	**1 2 3 4 5**
8	I feel that other students are better than me at speaking English.	**1 2 3 4 5**
9	I get so nervous in class that I forget everything.	**1 2 3 4 5**
10	I get nervous if I haven't prepared for English class.	**1 2 3 4 5**
11	I feel anxious even if I have prepared for English class.	**1 2 3 4 5**
12	I worry if the teacher corrects me in class.	**1 2 3 4 5**
13	The more I study English, the more I get confused.	**1 2 3 4 5**
14	I worry if I can't understand every word the teacher says.	**1 2 3 4 5**
15	I worry if my partner is better than me at English.	**1 2 3 4 5**
16	I get frustrated if my partner is not as good as me at English.	**1 2 3 4 5**
17	I worry about taking English tests.	**1 2 3 4 5**
18	I worry about failing the English course.	**1 2 3 4 5**
19	The English class makes me more nervous than other classes.	**1 2 3 4 5**
20	I often daydream in English class.	**1 2 3 4 5**

Comments:

Adapted from the *Foreign Language Classroom Anxiety Scale* (FLCAS), Horwitz, E. K. (1983).

LIFESTYLES (1)

- Our lifestyles reflect our learning preferences and our emotional needs.
- These are important influences on learning.
- Talk with a classmate about any of these topics:

Do you like sports?	Do you like fashion?	Do you like animals?
Are you a night-person?	What makes you happy?	What makes you unhappy?
Do you like to work with people?	Do you like to work with machines?	What is your favorite book?
What is your favorite food?	Are you energetic?	What can you do really well?
What can't you do?	Are you optimistic or pessimistic?	What is your favorite color?
Why are you studying English?	What do you like about yourself?	What do you dislike about yourself?
What is your best quality?	What is your worst quality?	What are your hobbies?
What do you do to relax?	What would you like to do in life?	What is your biggest worry?
What is your motto?	What clubs do you belong to?	How long do you sleep each night?
Do you like to travel in Korea?	What do you dream about?	What is your favorite day of the week?
Who is/was the greatest person ever?	Who is your favorite pop-star?	Who is your role-model?
What is your favorite piece of music?	Do you follow your heart or your brain?	Do you believe in destiny and fate?
Do you believe in God and the spirit?	Do you believe fortune tellers?	Do you believe in life after death?
How important are possessions?	How important is money?	How important is love?
What do you want to change in Korea?	What do you want to change in other people?	What do you want to change in yourself?

Adapted from *The Way Ahead*. Finch & Hyun (2000). Seoul: Hakmunsa, p. 38.

LIFESTYLES (2)

- **What is important in life?**
- **Choose** 5 questions from Lifestyles (1) [previous page).
- **Write** your 5 questions on this page.
- **Interview** your partner about your questions.
- **Write** your partner's answers on this page.

Question 1: ______

Answer: ______

Question 2: ______

Answer: ______

Question 3: ______

Answer: ______

Question 4: ______

Answer: ______

Question 5: ______

Answer: ______

Nine tenths of education is encouragement. (Anatole France)

Self-Assessment: Confidence

A positive self-image is very important:
- it helps us to focus on learning and meaning;
- it gives us strength to concentrate and understand;
- it encourages us to interact and communicate with others;
- it promotes motivation and positive attitudes.

My Self-Confidence Profile:	**False**		**Maybe**		**True**
1. I have the ability to learn English.	1	2	3	4	5
2. If I do my best, I will achieve my learning goals.	1	2	3	4	5
3. I will improve if I continue to study.	1	2	3	4	5
4. I like to speak in English in class.	1	2	3	4	5
5. Trying to speak English is more important than accuracy.	1	2	3	4	5
6. I like to study with my group members in class.	1	2	3	4	5
7. My contribution is as important as anyone else's.	1	2	3	4	5
8. I participate in all the activities in class.	1	2	3	4	5
9. I participate even if I am embarrassed or nervous.	1	2	3	4	5
10. I ask the teacher for help when needed.	1	2	3	4	5
11. If I don't understand, I say so.	1	2	3	4	5
12. I do my best, whatever the situation.	1	2	3	4	5
13. I keep trying to learn, even if I am nervous.	1	2	3	4	5
14. It is OK to make mistakes when practicing new language.	1	2	3	4	5
15. I'm not bothered what other students think of my efforts.	1	2	3	4	5
16. I'm not bothered what the teacher thinks of my efforts.	1	2	3	4	5
17. I believe in myself. I trust myself.	1	2	3	4	5
18. I trust my feelings and emotions.	1	2	3	4	5
19. I think about my learning ("How am I doing?").	1	2	3	4	5
20. I am a good language-learner.	1	2	3	4	5
TOTAL (/100)					

WHAT WOULD YOU TRY TO DO IF YOU KNEW YOU COULD NOT FAIL?

1. Circle the numbers that match your answers.
2. Add the numbers to make a total.
3. Take some time to think about your self-image:
   - *Do I respect myself?*
   - *Do I believe in my abilities?*
   - *Do I worry about what people think of me?*
   - *Do I trust myself to achieve my goals?*

My Reflections 8

- This is your journal page.
- You can write about anything here.
- Check out page 6 for suggestions.

Date: ____________________

Title:

Education is the art of making man ethical. (Georg Wilhelm Friedrich Hegel)

Strategy Inventory for Language Learning (1)

What are my learning strategies?

- Exchange books with a classmate.
- Imagine you are a government officer filling in an official form.
- Ask questions like a customs officer or immigration officer.
- Write the responses in your classmate's book.

Background Questionnaire

1. Name		2. Date		
3. Age	4. Gender	5. Mother tongue (L1)		

6. Language you speak at home

7. Language you are now learning

8. How long have you been learning the language in #7?

9. How do you rate your proficiency in the language in #7?

(Circle one of these):	Excellent	Good	Fair	Poor

10. How important is it for you to become proficient in the language in #7?

(Circle one):	Very Important	Important	Not Important

11. Why do you want to learn the language in #7?
.... I am interested in the language.
.... I am interested in the culture.
.... I have friends who speak the language
.... I am required to take a language course to graduate.
.... I need it for my future career.
.... I need it for travel.
.... Other (Please explain) ....
....

12. Do you enjoy language learning? (Circle one of these options):	Yes	No

13. What other languages have you studied?

14. What has been your favorite experience in language learning?
....
....
....

Adapted from: *SILL Version for Speakers of Other Languages Learning English. Version 7.0 (ESL/EFL).* R. L. Oxford, 1989.

Strategy Inventory for Language Learning (SILL) (2)

Now that you have finished the background questionnaire, you can ask about learning strategies. Explain the directions below, then work through the SILL with the other person.

On this page and the following page there are statements about learning English. Please read each statement. In the "1 - 5" column, write the response (1, 2, 3, 4, or 5) that tells HOW TRUE OF YOU THE STATEMENT IS.

1 = Never or almost never true of me.
2 = Usually not true of me.
3 = Somewhat true of me.
4 = Usually true of me.
5 = Always or almost always true of me.

1 - 5	#	SILL Part A (Remembering more effectively)
	1	I find relationships between what I already know and things I learn in English.
	2	I use new English words in a sentence so I can remember them.
	3	I connect the sound of a new English word with an image or picture of the word to help me remember the word.
	4	I remember a new English word by imagining a situation in which the word might be used.
	5	I use rhymes to remember new English words.
	6	I use flashcards to remember new English words.
	7	I physically act out new English words.
	8	I review English lessons often.
	9	I remember new English words or phrases by remembering their location on the page of the textbook, or on the board.

1 - 5	#	SILL Part B (Using all your mental processes)
	10	I say or write new English words several times.
	11	I try to talk like native English speakers.
	12	I practice the sounds of English.
	13	I use the English words I know in different ways.
	14	I start conversations in English.
	15	I watch English language TV shows or go to movies spoken in English.
	16	I read for pleasure in English.
	17	I write notes, messages, letters, or reports in English.
	18	I first skim an English passage then go back and read carefully.
	19	I look for words in Korean that are similar to new words in English.
	20	I try to find patterns in English words and phrases.
	21	I find the meaning of a word by dividing it into parts that I understand.
	22	I try not to translate word-for-word.
	23	I make summaries of information that I hear or read in English.

Strategy Inventory for Language Learning (SILL) (3)

Ask the other person to answer in terms of <u>how well the statement describes him/her.</u>

1 - 5	#	SILL Part C (Compensating for missing knowledge)
	24	I make guesses in order to understand unfamiliar English words.
	25	When I can't think of a word in English, I use gestures.
	26	I make up new words if I do not know the right ones in English.
	27	I read English without looking up every new word in the dictionary.
	28	I try to guess what the other person will say next in English.
	29	If I can't think of an English word, I use a word that means the same.

1 - 5	#	SILL Part D (Organizing and evaluating your learning)
	30	I try to find as many ways as I can to use my English.
	31	I notice my English mistakes and use that information to help me.
	32	I pay attention when someone is speaking in English.
	33	I try to find out how to be a better learner of English.
	34	I plan my schedule so I will have enough time to study English.
	35	I look for people I can talk to in English.
	36	I look for opportunities to read as much as possible in English.
	37	I have clear goals for improving my English skills.
	38	I think about my progress in learning English.

1 - 5	#	SILL Part E (Managing your emotions)
	39	I try to relax whenever I feel afraid of using English.
	40	I encourage myself to speak in English even if I am afraid of making a mistake.
	41	I give myself a reward or treat when I do well in English.
	42	I notice if I am tense or nervous when I am studying or using English.
	43	I write down my feelings in a language learning diary.
	44	I talk to someone else about how I feel when I am learning English.

1 - 5	#	SILL Part F (Learning with others)
	45	If I do not understand, I ask the speaker to slow down or say it again.
	46	I ask English speakers to correct me when I talk.
	47	I practice English with other students.
	48	I ask for help from English speakers.
	49	I ask questions in English.
	50	I try to learn about the culture of English speakers.

SILL (4)

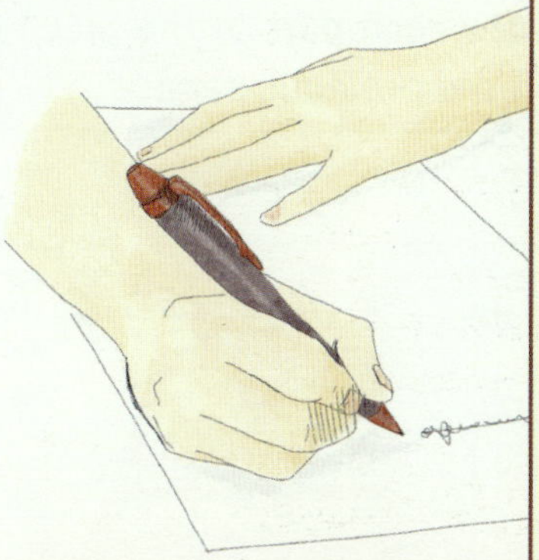

Worksheet for Answering and Scoring the SILL

1. The blanks in the table below are numbered for each item on the SILL.
2. Write the response to each item (1, 2, 3, 4, or 5) in each of the blanks.
3. Add up each column. Put the result in the box marked SUM.
4. Divide by the number under SUM to get the average for each column. Round this average off to the nearest tenth. E.g. 3.3578 = 3.4; 3.3429 = 3.3.
5. Figure out the overall average. To do this, add up all the SUMS for the different parts of the SILL. Then divide by 50.
6. When you have finished, copy the averages from the Worksheet onto the Profile of Results (next page).

SILL Part A		SILL Part B				SILL Part C		SILL Part D		SILL Part E		SILL Part F	
Q1		Q10		Q19		Q24		Q30		Q39		Q45	
Q2		Q11		Q20		Q25		Q31		Q40		Q46	
Q3		Q12		Q21		Q26		Q32		Q41		Q47	
Q4		Q13		Q22		Q27		Q33		Q42		Q48	
Q5		Q14		Q23		Q28		Q34		Q43		Q49	
Q6		Q15				Q29		Q35		Q44		Q50	
Q7		Q16						Q36					
Q8		Q17						Q37					
Q9		Q18						Q38					

SUM Part A:	SUM Part B:	SUM Part C:	SUM Part D:	SUM Part E:	SUM Part F:	A+B+C+ D+E+F =
SUM ÷9 (Average)	SUM ÷14 (Average)	SUM ÷6 (Average)	SUM ÷9 (Average)	SUM ÷6 (Average)	SUM ÷6 (Average)	A ~ F ÷50 (Average)

- Each part of the SILL (A to F) represents a group of learning strategies.
- The averages for each part show which groups of strategies you use most.
- The overall average tells you how often you use strategies for learning English.
- Use these scores on the next page.

SILL (5) Profile of Results

This Profile shows your SILL results. These results will tell you the kinds of strategies you use in learning English. To complete this profile, transfer your averages for each part of the SILL, and your overall average for the whole SILL. These averages are on the previous page.

Part	Learning Strategies	Averages
A	Remembering more effectively	
B	Using all your mental processes	
C	Compensating for missing knowledge	
D	Organizing and evaluating your learning	
E	Managing your emotions	
F	Learning with others	

Key to understanding your averages:		
High	Always or almost always used	**4.5 to 5.0**
	Usually used	**3.5 to 4.4**
Medium	Sometimes used	**2.5 to 3.4**
	Generally not used	**1.5 to 2.4**
Low	Never or almost never used	**1.0 to 1.4**

5.0							
4.5							
4.0							
3.5							
3.0							
2.5							
2.0							
1.5							
1.0							
	A: effective remembering	**B**: using all your mental processes	**C**: compensating for missing knowledge	**D**: organizing and evaluating learning	**E**: managing your emotions	**F**: learning with others	**A-F**: Overall average

Based on the *Version for Speakers of Other Languages Learning English. Version 7.0 (ESL/EFL)*. R. L. Oxford, 1989.

Call My Bluff (Team A)

(Team B: Next Page)

Speaker 1: Read your definition for **Pedagogic task.**
Speaker 2: Read your definition for **Pedagogic task.**
Speaker 3: Read your definition for **Pedagogic task.**
Everyone: Ask Team B to guess the correct meaning.
Only one definition is correct - which one is it?
Team A: Now listen to Team B reading their first word (Reliability).
Guess which definition is correct.
Write the correct definition at the bottom of the page.

Bluff-Words	Speaker 1's definitions
1. Pedagogic task	A form-focused task designed for language-learning inside the classroom.
2. Validity	The relationship between a test and the course content.
3. APS/VPS	Active Private Server/Virtual Private Server (Internet hosting)
4. Bottom-up learning	A focus on form, vocabulary and structure, leads finally to meaning.
5. Formative assessment	Students place themselves in their next class through self-assessment.
6. Affective filter	A method for streaming students into the most appropriate levels.

Bluff-Words	Speaker 2's definitions
1. Pedagogic task	A task included in an ELT teacher-training textbook.
2. Validity	The degree to which a test actually measures what it claims to measure.
3. APS/VPS	Actual Private Study/Virtual Private Study (Autonomy)
4. Bottom-up learning	A focus on meaning, without understanding all of the constituent parts.
5. Formative assessment	One-off tests which determine the next class or grade for the students.
6. Affective filter	A barrier to learning caused by negative emotional responses.

Bluff-Words	Speaker 3's definitions
1. Pedagogic task	A task which focuses on the theory of learning.
2. Validity	The influence which a test has on classroom teaching (preparation).
3. APS/VPS	Auditory Preference Style/Visual Preference Style.
4. Bottom-up learning	Educational reform by the government and the Ministry of Education.
5. Formative assessment	Feedback from activities is used to adapt teaching to the learners' needs.
6. Affective filter	Student-centered performance assessment (self/peer-assessment).

Team B's Words	(Write the correct definition)
1. Reliability	
2. Authentic task	
3. Procrastination	
4. Washback	
5. Plagiarism	
6. Apprehension	

Based on *The Way Ahead*. Finch & Hyun (2000). Seoul: Hakmunsa. p. 15.

Call My Bluff (Team B)

- **Listen to Team A reading their first word (Pedagogic task).**
- **Guess which definition is correct.**
- **Write the correct definition at the bottom of this page.**

 # Speaker 1: Read your definition of Reliability.
 # Speaker 2: Read your definition of Reliability.
 # Speaker 3: Read your definition of Reliability.
 # Everyone: Ask team A to guess the correct meaning.
Only one definition is correct - which one is it?

Bluff-Words	Speaker 1's definitions
1. Reliability	The extent to which a test uses real-world situations.
2. Authentic task	A task designed to promote emotional management as well as linguistic skills.
3. Procrastination	Excessive hesitation; taking a very long time to do something.
4. Washback	A method of monitoring rater-reliability in written and oral tests.
5. Plagiarism	The citation of another person's original work in an academic paper.
6. Apprehension	Perception on a direct and immediate level; intuitive understanding.

Bluff-Words	Speaker 2's definitions
1. Reliability	Consistency of results (for a test) over time and with different students.
2. Authentic task	A language-learning task which focuses on form rather than meaning.
3. Procrastination	A method of criterion-referenced testing.
4. Washback	The influence of classroom learning content on high stakes tests.
5. Plagiarism	The use or imitation of someone else's original work under one's own name.
6. Apprehension	Misunderstandings arising from inadequate interlanguage.

Bluff-Words	Speaker 3's definitions
1. Reliability	The accuracy of a test in terms of measuring what it is supposed to measure.
2. Authentic task	A language-learning task which uses real-world texts or situations.
3. Procrastination	The typical distribution curve of results in norm-referenced testing.
4. Washback	The effect that tests have on what gets taught in the classroom.
5. Plagiarism	Collaborative projects which feature presentations and written reports.
6. Apprehension	A type of higher-order thinking skill similar to inference.

Team A's Words	(Write the correct definition)
1. Pedagogic task	
2. Validity	
3. APS/VPS	
4. Bottom-up learning	
5. Formative assessment	
6. Affective filter	

Based on *The Way Ahead*. Finch & Hyun (2000). Seoul: Hakmunsa. p. 16.

Learner-Counseling: Role Play (2)

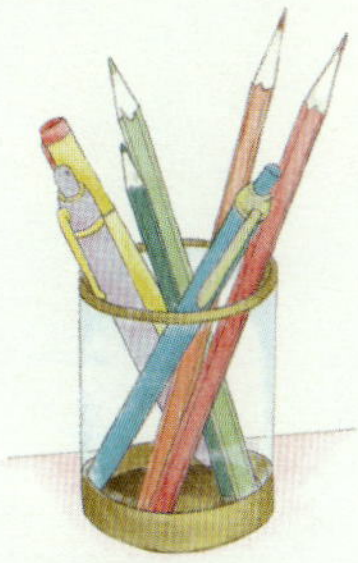

Groups (4 people): Try this role play.

- Use the cards on this page as hints - starting points.
- Have some deep discussion between teacher and students.
- Use your imagination - be creative!

Teacher

You have asked some students to come to your office. You wish to discuss some compositions (final assignments) which have been handed in by them:

- Student A) is an excellent student, but his/her composition is not as good as usual.
- Student B) is a bully. You suspect that he/she has forced A) to write his/her compositions.
- Student C) usually works hard, but this time his/her composition was terrible .

Student A)

The teacher has asked you to visit his/her office to discuss your composition.

- You had to help Student B) by writing his/her composition, or he/she would have hit you.
- Why does the teacher have to interfere?
- Everyone in class will call you teacher's pet if Student B) is punished.
- What will you say to the teacher?

Student B)

The teacher has asked you to visit his/her office to discuss your composition.

- The teacher is always rude to you and makes fun of you in class.
- How can you be motivated in this situation?
- What's the use of doing your best? The teacher will not give you good grades.
- What will you say to the teacher?

Student C)

The teacher has asked you to visit his/her office to discuss your composition.

- Doesn't the teacher know that your father is in hospital?
- You have to look after the family while your mother is at work.
- You have a part-time job, to pay for the hospital fees.
- What will you say to the teacher?

Well done! How about performing your role play to the other groups?
How about making a different role play?

2-Minute Discussion: Learning to Learn

- **Make** two lines of chairs, facing each other.
- **Give** one discussion topic to each student.
- **Discuss** the topics in pairs for two minutes.
- **Everybody** stand up and move one chair to your left.
- **Discuss** topics with new partners (2 minutes).

What is the best way to learn a second language?

How are your cognitive thinking skills now?

What do you expect from the teacher?

How are your performance skills?

Tell me about your preferred learning methods.

How are your Critical-thinking skills?

Tell me about a learning experience you had.

How autonomous are you as a learner?

Can you assess yourself? How is your progress?

Tell me about your Multiple Intelligences.

What do you remember about middle school?

How is this school preparing you for the future?

What sort of learner are you (Visual, Auditory, Tactile)?

Tell me about your learning role model.

My Reflections 9

- This is your journal page.
- You can write about anything here.
- Check out page 6 for suggestions.

Date: ____________________

Title:

The simplest way to ensure that students expect success is to make sure that they achieve it consistently. (Jere Brophy)

What Should I Do?

1. Choose one problem on this page. ➤➤➤ 2. Ask the people in your group for advice.
3. Who gave you the best advice? ➤➤➤ 4. Write this advice in the "Best Advice" box.

Asking for advice:
I have no idea what to do.
I'm between a rock and a hard place.
What would you do if you were me?

Giving advice:
If I were you, I would ...
Why don't you ...?
How about ...ing?
In your place, I would ...
You could always ...
Have you thought about ...?

I want to be a doctor, but I don't like studying English. What should I do? Is there an alternative?

I want to become an English teacher. How should I spend my study time? Please advise me.

I'm not motivated to study these days. Everything seems too difficult. Whatever I do, I can't succeed. What should I do? Should I give up?

I'm worried that I will fail the course. My grades are low and I don't understand what the English teacher says. What should I do?

I have an important exam next week, but I have no time to study for it because of my part-time job. What should I do?

My girlfriend/boyfriend wants to go to America to study, but I have to get a high score in TOEFL if I want to follow him/her. What should I do?

I want to study for the teachers' exam, but my friends keep inviting me to go out with them instead. They say that it's no use trying to pass the exam. What should I do?

I want to teach children and encourage a love of learning in them, but I don't want to teach the sort of test-preparation that I experienced in school. What should I do?

I can't afford the school tuition fees or the books. If I want to continue studying, I must get a job and earn money. I also want to send money to my parents. What should I do?

Best advice:

____

____

____

____

____

____

____

____

____

____

____

Based on *Now You're Talking*. Finch & Hyun (2000). Seoul: Hakmunsa. p. 96.

Share the Wealth

- Your school has received a $5,000 donation .
- Your group must decide on how to spend that money.
- Your group must agree 100% on the choice.

During this activity, practice effective listening skills:

Options for spending the money:

1. Divide the money equally among all the class members.
2. Use the money to pay for a field trip for a class project.
3. Give the money to the Education Department for educational resources.
4. Use the money to buy toys for local poor children and orphans.
5. Donate the money to an organization that provides meals for beggars.
6. Use the money to buy blankets and give them to homeless people.
7. Use the money to set up a recycling program to help save the environment.
8. Use the money to set up a scholarship for poor students.
9. Spend the money on a fun party for the class.
10. Your own idea.

S Be **S**till; be **S**ilent

H **H**ear what others are saying.
Hear what they mean.

A **A**llow others to speak.
Accept what the others say as true for them.
Pay **A**ttention.

R **R**estate what you heard the other person say, to be sure you understand.

E **E**ncourage others to speak.

KINDNESS
Pass it on!

Give a flower Eat lunch with someone new
Listen with your heart Visite a sick friend
Clean a neighbor's walk Offer a hug
Give an unexpected gift Make a new friend
Pick up litter Say "hello" Call a lonely student
Open a Door Help carry a load Plant a tree
Pass a kindness on Share a snack
Cheer up a friend Thank a Teacher Lend a hand
Read to a young child Do a kind act daily
Leave a thank you note Offer your seat
Cycle courteously BE TOLERANT Let another go first
Bake cookies for firefighters Give a compliment
Help a student make friends Assist an adult
Give a balloon away Lend a classmate a pencil
Celebrate something every day Encourage a friend
Respect others Walk a dog Do a favor
Forgive mistakes Smile at someone new

www.actsofkindness.org

Purpose

This activity emphasizes the importance of working together, learning to cooperate rather than compete. Students learn to communicate better, especially to listen to each other's viewpoints, if they learn to trust each other and to solve problems together. In this way, ignorance can be replaced with knowledge, insecurity with confidence, and fear with love.

Adapted from *Educating the Heart*. Siccone & López (2000). pp. 191 – 194.

Learning Contract

Groups of 4 people: Do you remember the Pre-Nuptial Agreement (page 52)? Let's make a similar contract - about our English classes.

- Think about learning needs, goals, assessment, and study methods.
- What do we need to do to make this course as helpful (and enjoyable) as possible for us?

Learning Contract

We, the undersigned, have agreed on the following conditions for our English class.
We will try to keep these conditions at all times.

In our English classes ...

1. ***We should ....***
2. ***We should ....***
3. ***We should ....***
4. ***We should ....***
5. ***The teacher should ....***
6. ***The teacher should ....***
7. ***We should not ....***
8. ***We should not ....***
9. ***We should not ....***
10. ***The teacher should not ....***

Signed by ....

..

Witnessed by ....

Date ....

Adapted from *The Way Ahead*. Finch & Hyun (2000). Seoul: Hakmunsa, p. 18.

Learner-Counseling: Role Play (3)

Groups (4 people): Try this role play. Let's have some deep discussion between teacher and parents:

- What do they want for their children?
- What do they need from the teacher?
- Do they know the true situation in the class?
- Can you resolve their fears and worries?

Teacher: You have asked some parents to come to your office to discuss their sons or daughters, who have been having some problems lately:

- **Parent A**: The daughter is an excellent student, but she seems unmotivated and lazy these days. Is there a problem at home?
- **Parent B**: The son spends much of class sleeping on the desk. He is obviously exhausted. What does the parent say about this?
- **Parent C**: The son often picks fights with other students. The others treat him as an outsider and he seems to have no friends. Does the parent know about this?

Parent A:

The teacher has asked you to visit his/her office to discuss your daughter.

- What's the problem? You do everything for your daughter.
- You give her everything she asks for.
- If there is a problem at school, it must be the teacher's fault.
- What will you say to the teacher?

Parent B:

The teacher has asked you to visit his/her office to discuss your son.

- What's going on here? You hope your son is going to get good grades.
- He goes to the library every night, and sleeps there after studying.
- You are proud of him. What will you say to the teacher?

Parent C:

The teacher has asked you to visit his/her office to discuss your son.

- You are worried about your son.
- He tells you that other students are picking fights with him.
- This has to stop. The teacher should take care of your son.
- What will you say to the teacher?

Perform your role play to the other groups.
How about making a video of your role play?
How about making a different role play?

My Reflections 10

- This is your journal page.
- You can write about anything here.
- Check out page 6 for suggestions.

Date: ____________________

Title: ____________________

Education must be not only a transmission of culture but also a provider of alternative views of the world and a strengthener of the will to explore them. (Jerome S. Bruner)

Computer-Assisted Language Learning (CALL)

Here are some ideas about teaching a foreign language with the help of computers.
Circle the number that matches your opinion:

1 = I agree strongly with this statement.
2 = I agree on the whole with this statement.
3 = I neither agree nor disagree with this statement.
4 = I disagree on the whole with this statement.
5 = I disagree strongly with this statement.

Discuss these issues with your group members.

Statement					
We can teach foreign languages through the Internet.	1	2	3	4	5
We can teach grammar through computer software.	1	2	3	4	5
We can teach vocabulary using computers.	1	2	3	4	5
We can teach pronunciation through computer software.	1	2	3	4	5
We can teach communication through the Internet.	1	2	3	4	5
We can develop all 4 language skills with computers.	1	2	3	4	5
Language teachers should use social networking sites in their classes.	1	2	3	4	5
Language teachers should use virtual reality sites.	1	2	3	4	5
Language teachers should make their own websites.	1	2	3	4	5
Language students should play online language games.	1	2	3	4	5
Language students should chat online in the target language.	1	2	3	4	5
Teachers should use Blogs to encourage writing in English.	1	2	3	4	5
Teachers should use Wikis to encourage writing in English.	1	2	3	4	5
Language courses should include computer lessons.	1	2	3	4	5
Teachers should make Webquests to encourage project-work.	1	2	3	4	5
Computers will replace books in language classes.	1	2	3	4	5
Computers will replace teachers in language classes.	1	2	3	4	5
The Internet will replace classrooms. Students will study from home.	1	2	3	4	5
The Internet is a good source of language teaching materials.	1	2	3	4	5
The Internet is good for students who want to study by themselves.	1	2	3	4	5

CALL/MALL Board Game

How can we use CALL and Multimedia-Assisted Language Learning to teach English?

- Play this game in groups.
- When you land on a square, explain how you would use CALL and MALL to teach this aspect of English. (What? Why? How?)
- Follow the ladders going up.

Software for the Language Classroom

Here are some ideas about using software to teach English.

- **Draw** a cross (X) at the point on each continuum that matches your opinion.
- **Discuss** the ideas with people in your group.
- **Make** a mark (e.g. Θ) at the points that match your group's opinion.
- **Change** groups. Discuss with the new group.

Ideas, beliefs and perceptions about language learning software and the Internet:

Presentation software like *PowerPoint* is a great teaching tool for language teachers.

I/we agree with this statement. ⟷ I/we disagree with this statement.

Spreadsheet software like *EXCEL* is invaluable for keeping records and for assessment.

I/we agree with this statement. ⟷ I/we disagree with this statement.

Every teacher should learn how to use Database software such as *ACCESS.*

I/we agree with this statement. ⟷ I/we disagree with this statement.

Graphic software such as *Photoshop* is very helpful for language teachers.

I/we agree with this statement. ⟷ I/we disagree with this statement.

Teachers should learn how to use crossword and wordsearch software.

I/we agree with this statement. ⟷ I/we disagree with this statement.

Teachers should learn how to use language game software.

I/we agree with this statement. ⟷ I/we disagree with this statement.

Teachers should be able to use HTML software such as *HTML Kit.*

I/we agree with this statement. ⟷ I/we disagree with this statement.

Virtual reality sites are very useful for developing speaking skills.

I/we agree with this statement. ⟷ I/we disagree with this statement.

Teachers should be able to use Blogs and Wikis.

I/we agree with this statement. ⟷ I/we disagree with this statement.

Language teachers should make their own websites or *Facebook* sites.

I/we agree with this statement. ⟷ I/we disagree with this statement.

Phone-text spelling is destroying the English language.

I/we agree with this statement. ⟷ I/we disagree with this statement.

There is too much technology these days. It is not helpful to language learning.

I/we agree with this statement. ⟷ I/we disagree with this statement.

Discussion:
The Internet and Language Learning

Everyone: Ask these questions to your partner or to other people in your group. Talk about your Internet habits, routines and preferences. Is the Internet really good for language learning?

Would you like an e-pal (email friend)? (Why? Why not?)

Have you ever used social networking sites (e.g. Facebook)?

How often do you use a computer? (Every hour/evening/day/week, etc.)

What do you use computers for? (Browsing, word processing, chatting, email, etc.)

Do you use the Internet to study English?

Have you ever played language games on the Internet?

Have you ever downloaded language-learning software from the Internet?

How can teachers use the Internet for the English classroom?

What are your favourite Internet sites?

Have you ever read newspapers on the Internet?

Have you ever visited a library on the Internet?

Have you ever visited the website of the BBC? CNN? ABC? NBC?

Have you ever tried an interactive English quiz on the Internet?

Have you ever looked for song lyrics and movie scripts on the Internet?

My Reflections 11

- This is your journal page.
- You can write about anything here.
- Check out page 6 for suggestions.

Date: ____________________

Title:

Education becomes a meaningless endeavor unless the education acquired has some impact on the human condition. (Pine & Boy, 1977)

Self-Assessment (continued on the next page)

Exchange books with a classmate.
Ask about his/her speaking ability. e.g. Can you greet somebody?

- If he/she says "Yes, I can", ask him/her to prove it!
- e.g. Really? Please show me. (Look at the examples.)

Language Functions and Examples	Yes, 100%	Yes, 50%	No
1. I can greet somebody in English. *e.g. Hello. How do you do?*			
2. I can take leave of somebody in English. *e.g. Good night. See you again. It was nice talking with you.*			
3. I can give personal information in English. *e.g. My name is ... I am Korean. I come from ...*			
4. I can ask for personal information in English. *e.g. How old are you? Where do you come from? What's your surname?*			
5. I can ask for the time in English. *e.g. What time is it?*			
6. I can give the time to someone. *e.g. It's half past three.*			
7. I can ask for directions. *e.g. Could you tell me the way to ...?*			
8. I can give directions to someone. *e.g. Turn left at the church. It's next to the bank. First turning on your left.*			
9. I can ask for information. *e.g. When is the next bus? Where is it?*			
10. I can say my phone number without having to think about it. *e.g. Zero, three, dash, five, four, seven ...*			
11. I can communicate on the phone. *e.g. I'd like to speak to Mr. Smith. Is Mr. Smith there? When will he be back?*			
12. I can answer a phone call. *e.g. Who's calling? Would you like to leave a message? Shall I tell him you called?*			
13. I can give instructions. *e.g. Open the door. Please stand up.*			
14. I can ask for help. *e.g. Can you help me?*			
15. I can agree with someone. *e.g. I agree with you. Yes, you're right.*			
16. I can disagree with someone. *e.g. I can't agree with you.*			
17. I can make an invitation. *e.g. Would you like to go to the movies?*			
18. I can decline an invitation. *e.g. No, thank you. Sorry, I have an appointment.*			
19. I can offer to help. *e.g. Can I help you? Shall I carry your bags?*			
20. I can ask for permission to do something. *e.g. Is it OK to park here? Do you mind if I smoke? May I open the window?*			
21. I can make an appointment. *e.g. Are you free tomorrow?*			
22. I can make an excuse. *e.g. I'm sorry, I'm too busy.*			

Self-Assessment

Language Functions and Examples	Yes, 100%	Yes, 50%	No
23. I can make a reservation. *e.g. I'd like a ticket to Seoul. A table for two please. Are there any seats for tonight's concert?*			
24. I can talk about things I like. *e.g. I like kimchi. Movies turn me on.*			
25. I can talk about things I don't like. *e.g. I hate hot-dogs.*			
26. I can talk about my favorite things. *e.g. I love reading comics.*			
27. I can compare things. *e.g. I am older than my sister. Learning English is more difficult than learning Japanese.*			
28. I can talk about preferences. *e.g. I prefer Soju to Dong-dong-ju.*			
29. I can describe people. *e.g. She is of medium height with curly hair.*			
30. I can use conditionals (if – then). *e.g. If it rains then I'll go home. If I were rich then I would travel.*			
31. I can ask about plans. *e.g. How long will you stay?*			
32. I can apologize. *e.g. I'm really sorry. Please forgive me.*			
33. I can give advice. *e.g. If I were you ...... Why don't you ......?*			
34. I can give warnings. *e.g. Look out! Be careful!*			
35. I can ask for opinions. *e.g. What do you think? What's your opinion?*			
36. I can talk about my feelings. *e.g. I'm happy. I feel down.*			
37. I can complain. *e.g. This food is cold. You're late!*			
38. I can express sympathy. *e.g. I'm sorry to hear that. What a shame.*			
39. I can ask about experiences. *e.g. Have you ever been to Busan? Have you ever seen a ghost? Have you ever fallen in love?*			
40. I can express dissatisfaction. *e.g. I'm not happy with this CD player.*			
41. I can express disappointment. *e.g . I expected more of you.*			
42. I can be polite in all situations. *e.g. Please control yourself.*			
43. I can express anger appropriately. *e.g. How dare you say that?*			
44. I can use formal language correctly. *e.g. Ladies and gentlemen. It gives me great pleasure to be here today.*			
45. I can tell a joke in English. *e.g. A) Hello, doctor. I think I'm losing my memory. B) When did you first notice this? A) Notice what?*			
46. I can use sarcasm in English. *e.g. Would you like some tea with your sugar?*			
47. I can use English idioms. *e.g. I'll take a rain-check on that party tonight.*			

Adapted from Oskarsson, M. (1980). *Approaches to Self-assessment in Foreign Language Learning*. Council of Europe: Pergamon Press.

Highlights of My Life (1)

Groups: This activity helps you to picture the future.
It is a good idea to play quiet music with this activity!

- We all have our own strengths and talents.
- We can all make successful careers and lives.
- Visualizing the future helps us to choose success.

Student A: Read the words below (slowly) to the other students.
Other Students: Listen to Student A.

Close your eyes. Take some deep breaths. Imagine yourself walking down a long hallway that feels like home. At the end of the hallway is a room just like the one you've always wanted. As you enter the room, you see your favorite colors on the walls, and your favorite things in the room. This is a perfect place to be.

You relax for a while on a sofa. You decide to watch TV. As you watch, a movie comes on. It is called "A Life." It is divided into three parts: i) your past; ii) the next five years; and iii) the five years after that.

You see the highlights of your past life. As you watch, the events of the next five years unfold. Now you move further into the future, to 6 - 10 years from now. Excellent! You notice the high points of these years.

The movie is over. You turn off the TV and leave the room. You enter this classroom and sit in your chair. You can feel your back against the back of the chair, and your feet on the floor. You slowly open your eyes and look around the room.

Everyone: Ask yourself: "What have I done in my life so far?"

Stage 1: In the first row of film frames (next page), draw three important events in your life so far.

Stage 2: Now ask yourself "What do I want to do in the next five years?" In the second row of film frames (next page), draw three events you hope to experience in the next five years.

Stage 3: Next ask yourself "What do I want to do in the five years after that?" In the third row of film frames, draw 3 events for the next 5 years.

Stage 4: Share your filmstrips with your group members.

Based on Finch & Sampson (2004). *It's Up to You*. Seoul: Chonghab Publishing, pp. 263-264.

Highlights of My Life (2)

First row of film frames

Second row of film frames

Third row of film frames

Final Learning Contract

- Groups of 4 people
- We're coming to the end of the Learning Journal.
- Let's make a Lifelong Learning Contract.
- What do we want to do after this course?
- How will we continue learning for life?

One of the most important skills in the 21st century is the ability to acquire new skills. Change is a constant aspect of our lives, and we need to learn new things all the time. We, the undersigned, have therefore decided that we will take the following actions for lifelong learning.

1. We will ______________________________
2. We won't ______________________________
3. We should ______________________________
4. We shouldn't ______________________________
5. We must ______________________________
6. We mustn't ______________________________
7. We ought to ______________________________
8. We oughtn't to ______________________________
9. We hope to ______________________________
10. We hope not to ______________________________

Signatures: ______________________________

Date: ______________________________

Based on *The Way Ahead*. Finch & Hyun (2000). Seoul: Hakmunsa. p. 18.

Review and final discussion

We have reflected on many aspects of teaching and learning in this journal.
We have also written many *Reflections*. Let's reflect on our *Reflections*.

- Look at the graphics below. What do they mean to you?
- Discuss the concepts behind the graphics.

A Letter to Myself

1. WRITE a letter: (FROM "me" TO "me").
2. Put it in an envelope.
3. Write YOUR address on the envelope.
4. Give the letter to the teacher.
5. The teacher will send you this letter ONE YEAR LATER!
6. You will read this letter NEXT YEAR!

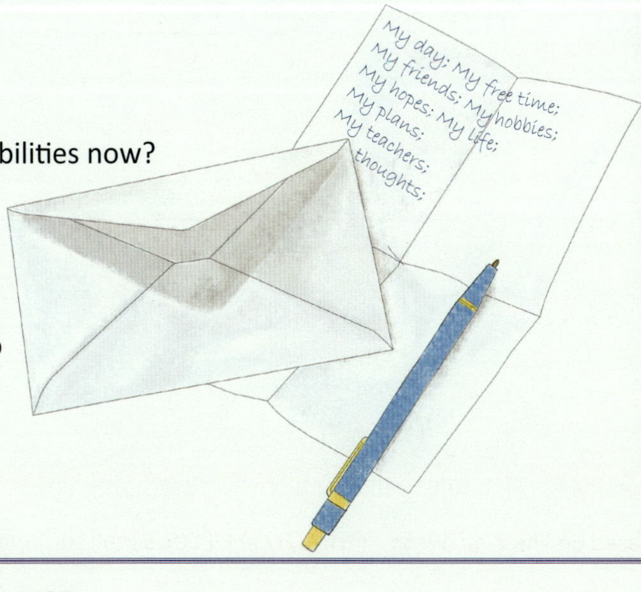

- What will you write about?
- How do you feel about your learning abilities now?
- How do you feel about yourself now?
- Are you more confident?
- Are you more motivated?
- Are you an independent learner?
- Has this learning journal helped you to think about education?

My Final Reflections

- This is your final journal page.
- You can write about anything here.
- How do you feel, now that the course is nearly over?

Date: ____________________

Title:

You can learn new things at any time in your life if you're willing to be a beginner.
If you actually like being a beginner, the whole world opens up to you. (Barbara Sher)

Feedback: What Did I Learn?

Feedback is important for learning. It helps us to:
- improve courses and journals;
- design courses to suit student needs;
- offer advice on learning to students;
- assess ourselves and the courses;
- evaluate course success and appropriateness.

Fill in this table with ideas about your learning.	**My Comments**
1. Did this journal help me develop my English skills?	
2. Did this journal help me become more confident about my English skills and abilities?	
3. Did this journal help me become more motivated about learning English?	
4. Did this journal help me to express my ideas in English?	
5. Did this journal help me improve my learning skills? Did I learn how to learn?	
6. Did this journal help me become more autonomous? Can I continue learning English by myself?	
7. Did I learn about collaboration while doing this journal? How did I get on with other learners ?	
8. Did my ideas about language learning and teaching change while doing this journal?	
9. Did my ideas and perceptions about myself and my abilities change while doing this journal?	
10. How can this journal be improved?	

Teacher's Thoughts

- Well done for all your efforts!
- Now give your journal to the teacher.
- The teacher will give you some feedback on this page.
- Please reflect on this feedback and use it to help you make some new learning goals and plans.

Date: ____________________

Title: ____

Warm-hearted interaction between teachers and learners, as well as among the learners themselves is, in our opinion, the most essential factor in successful language learning.
(M. Sano, M. Takahashi, & A. Yoneyama)

Socratic Dialogs and Discussions*

1. Education
2. Assessment
3. Testing
4. The Classroom
5. Self-Assessment
6. Learned Helplessness
7. Collaboration
8. Journals
9. Performance Assessment
10. Portfolios
11. Rewards
12. The Internet
13. Bear Makes a Test
14. A Model Lesson

* Except for the first two, the Socratic dialogs in this section first appeared in *Integrating Teaching and Assessment in the EFL Classroom: A Practical Guide for Teachers in Korea*, Finch, A. E. & Shin, Dongil (2005), Sahoipyungnon Publishing Co. Inc., and are reprinted here with permission.

Socratic Dialog (1): Education

We are visiting (Ms.) Tiger and (Mr.) Bear in the mountains of Korea. Bear is new to foreign language teaching and is very confused. Tiger has seen ideas come and go, and has evolved her own ideas from experience.

Scene: Bear arrives at Tiger's cave, just as Tiger is preparing ginseng tea.

Tiger: Hello Bear. Good to see you. Would you like some Insam cha with wild bee honey? (*Bear sits down in the most comfortable chair, next to the fire.*)

Bear: Thank you, Tiger. That would be nice. But this isn't just a social call. I'm sorry to trouble you, but I need your help.

Tiger: Of course. What can I do for you?

Bear: I have to write an essay on education, but I don't know where to start.

Tiger: (*Pouring tea into Bear's cup*) Believe it or not, Bear, this topic can be surprisingly interesting.

Bear: It's OK for you, Tiger. You don't have to do the writing.

Tiger: (*Holding the sugar bowl*) Do you take one lump of sugar or two? I can't remember. Well, Bear, if you go back to philosophers such as Plato, Aristotle and Confucius, you will find that they talk about education in terms of the human condition. Education for them was a means of producing and preserving a caring society. More recently, philosophers such as Bernard Shaw, H.G. Wells, and Krishnamurti have seen education as the only thing that can prevent the self-destruction of the human species.

Bear: Come on, Tiger! I'm not a philosopher. My job is to teach language. Two lumps, please.

Tiger: You make an interesting observation, Bear. But the literature has been telling us for a long time that students do not learn what they are taught. Hence, it is paradoxical that teachers continue to teach in a manner that they know does not work. The database for content and information has exploded, but the same old teaching ideas remain. "More" does not mean "better." Students leave the classroom at the end of the semester with pretty much the same level of skills they had on the first day. Everyone (including you) is frustrated and disappointed.

Bear: Stop using all these long words Tiger, and just tell me: What is learning? What is teaching?

Tiger: One step at a time, dear friend. Would you like some mountain-strawberry jam? I made it myself. Don't worry. I used honey from wild bees instead of sugar.

Bear: Now you're talking! I love your jam. (*Bear helps himself to toast and jam.*)

Tiger: The fact that you ask these questions, Bear, indicates that you believe that learning and teaching can be simply defined and then objectively tested. Let me ask you a question. Why is the factory model of mass education, which has been going on since the Industrial Revolution, viewed by everyone as a failure?

Bear: I told you Tiger, I'm a language teacher, not a politician. This jam is delicious!

Tiger: Like it or not, Bear, you'll have to look at this problem sometime. Philosophers see the lack of social responsibility in students, politicians see the lack of academic success, employers see the lack of applied critical thinking skills, parents see the lack of human values, and students see the lack of meaning in the things they have been taught. Even students who are "successful" are typically unable to apply their knowledge in real life. As Carl Rogers said in the 1950s, education "from the neck up" has produced terrible results. It is time to educate the emotions and the feelings.

Bear: What do you mean, Tiger?

Tiger: Think about it, Bear. Are you educating your students to become responsible, caring, sharing, problem-solving, critical-thinking citizens? Or are you simply teaching them to pass the university entrance test, the iBT TOEFL, the IELTS, or the TOEIC test? Are you an educator, or an education-factory worker?

Bear: I have no choice, Tiger. If my students don't pass the test, I lose my job.

Tiger: I understand, Bear, but have you considered that if your students were learning English because they enjoyed it, if they were using English to perform meaningful and authentic tasks in your classroom, or if they were actively following an extensive reading program of their own volition, then their English skills might be much better than they are now?

Bear: I'd love to try these things, Tiger, but I'm afraid it can't be done.

Tiger: Yes, it can, Bear, and you have a responsibility to do it. The real values of education must be present in every class, including yours. More tea?

(More next time ...)

Discussion questions

1. What are the goals of education?
   - How can these goals be achieved?
   - Are these goals being achieved now?
2. What are the goals of language education?
   - How can these goals be achieved?
   - Are these goals being achieved now?
3. Do you agree with Tiger?
   - Why? Why not?
4. What are 'affective filters'?
   - How do they affect learning?
5. How do perceptions affect teaching and learning?
6. How does motivation affect teaching and learning?

Socratic Dialog (2): Assessment

We are still with Tiger and Bear in the mountains of Korea.
They are taking a mountain stroll, reading books.

Bear looks up from his book and asks Tiger a question.

Bear: What's all this fuss about testing, Tiger? This book says we shouldn't test students. But everyone knows we have to test them to find their language level.

Tiger: Look at that tree, Bear. Do you think it knows that it is a tree? Is it aware?

Bear: Please don't change the subject, Tiger.

Tiger: I wasn't, actually. But before I answer, can you tell me what a language test is?

Bear: Of course, Tiger. A language test is a way of finding out whether students understand the structure of the language and can use it in real-life situations.

Tiger: I see. So the two main factors are comprehension and performance?

Bear: Well, there are lots of other factors, but communicative competence is important.

Tiger: Excuse me for asking, Bear, but how do you measure this competence? (*looks up*) What a beautiful butterfly!

Bear: Well, Tiger, we use internationally accepted performance criteria. For example: we consider **R**ange, **E**ase of Speech, **A**ccuracy, **D**elivery, and **I**nteraction, in the case of speaking tests.

Tiger: Yes, I've heard of these **READI** criteria. But you haven't told me <u>how</u> you measure language. (*The butterfly lands on Tiger's nose.*)

Bear: That's simple. We ask two teachers to rate the performance of each student.

Tiger: I don't want to disillusion you, Bear, but your results depend on how the rater feels that day, how the students feel, and lots of other considerations. (*The butterfly flies off and Tiger picks up a pine cone.*)

Bear: I know, Tiger. I've often thought that we are testing performance skills rather than language ability. But what else can we do?

Tiger: (*Studying the pine cone.*) How about using Classroom-Based Assessment?

Bear: Well, I've read about it, but I don't think there's any way I could use it.

Tiger: Believe it or not, Bear, Classroom-Based Assessment could be extremely helpful in your class. You are testing language code (grammar), and performance skills. How do you deal with students who don't like performing? How do you deal with anxiety, stress, peer-pressure, parental pressure, negative attitudes, fear of failure, and lack of confidence? What do you say to the student who can't stay awake during your test because his/her parents had an argument last night? All these factors affect your test results.

Bear: Sorry, Tiger. There's nothing I can do. These things are beyond my control. (*Bear drinks from a cool mountain stream.*)

Tiger: So you continue to give tests which have nothing to do with education of the individual, with holistic learning, with emotional growth, or with social responsibility. Really, Bear, your students are getting very little out of this test.

Bear: I have to give grades, Tiger.

Tiger: Open your mind, Bear. Respect your students as thinking human beings. Students should assess themselves. They are the people who need the information from testing so that they can manage their learning goals and plans.

Bear: Come on, Tiger, you know that they will all cheat if I let them assess each other.

Tiger: If you don't trust them, and if you don't respect them, then they will cheat. However, if you give them responsibility to assess themselves on weekly tests, they will make the tests, mark them, and discuss how to make them better. During this time, they will be thinking about the learning process, and will be making great steps in the direction of self-directed learning and social responsibility. You will really be helping your students, Bear.

Bear: Give me a break, Tiger. This would take months of planning. I don't have the time.

Tiger: It will actually save you time, Bear, and your students will be more motivated and aware of the learning process. Start using continuous assessment, like portfolios, learning journals and projects. Trust your students. Let them assess themselves and each other. Involve them in evaluation. You will be surprised with the results. Now, let's go home. It's time for tea.

(More next time ...)

Discussion questions

1. What are the goals of assessment?
   - How can these goals be achieved?
   - Are these goals being achieved now?
2. How can we assess the four macros skills (reading, listening, speaking, writing)?
3. What are learning styles?
   - How can we assess them?
4. What are learning strategies?
   - How can we assess them?
5. How can we assess affective factors such as attitude, confidence, motivation, anxiety, and stress?
6. Can students assess themselves?
7. Can we really involve students in assessment?

Socratic Dialog (3): Testing

Scene: Bear and Tiger have returned to Tiger's cave for some tea and crumpets. The debate continues.

Tiger: Ah, here we are. It's nice to be home again. I can't wait to make a cup of tea.

Bear: Absolutely, Tiger. The fresh air has given me a good appetite for tea and some of those lovely crumpets you make.

Tiger: Of course. I'll make some straight away. Now, what were we talking about?

Bear: I was saying that tests are unavoidable. We have to know what has been learned, so that we can predict future learning, and recommend students for universities and jobs.

Tiger: That's right. I remember now. You have made many interesting observations today, Bear. Unfortunately, we must face facts. Our testing culture and all-out competition for grades has borne bitter fruit. The very clear message that we are giving the students is that if you remember the correct facts and perform well on a handful of dates, everything will be OK. This is not a useful state of mind to take into professional or personal life. Now where did I put the Earl Grey teabags?

Bear: I think they're on the shelf to your left.
Do you mean that our testing system isn't really helping students to prepare for life?

Tiger: You took the words right out of my mouth, Bear. A school test-driven environment has nothing to do with the real world needs of students. Employers want team-workers. They also want problem-solvers, and people who can come up with creative ideas. Our tests should be evaluating higher-order thinking skills and communicative abilities. Society needs thinking human beings, not memory machines.

Bear: Now I know you're joking, Tiger. Look at all the recent fuss about communicative language teaching. The results are just the same as they have always been.

Tiger: Well done, Bear. I think you're beginning to wake up. People tried to solve the situation a generation or so ago, and came up with the concept of 'learner-centered' teaching. Here you are. A cup of Earl Grey tea and your favorite crumpets.

Bear: Wonderful. Thank you, Tiger. But don't stop. Please go on.

Tiger: Oh, yes. Great steps were taken in the field of ELT and tremendous thought was given to a brave new world of happy, productive classrooms.

Bear: So where are the results, 20 years down the road?

Tiger: The truth is Bear, all the benefits of task-based learning and learner independence were just crammed into conventional, teacher-controlled practices. Instead of trying out the new ideas, teachers carried on with their usual teaching practices, but renamed them as "communicative" or "task-based."

Bear: You mean "Old wine in new bottles?" You paint a sad picture, Tiger. But what can be done?

Bear: Should teachers and students all continue pushing the big, rough rock of Sisyphus[1) semester after semester?

Tiger: Let us look at the facts. SLA experts have told us that acquiring a second language is probably the most complex cognitive act we perform as adults. They have also told us that traditional teacher-controlled methods have no justification in theory or in practice.

Bear: So how does all this fit into my classroom practice in Korea?

Tiger: Check out the website of the Ministry of Education. You will find that the official goal of education in Korea is education of the whole person, rather than the exam-driven hell that teachers and students complain about. Here's a quote from the site: "Korean education has established humanization, refinement, informativeness, human welfare and open-mindedness as its ultimate goals. Various efforts are being made to raise a self-reliant individual equipped with a distinct sense of independence, a creative individual with a sense of originality, and an ethical individual with some sound morality and democratic ideology."

Bear: I see what you mean, Tiger. There is nothing here about memory-based, multiple-choice testing of rote-learned facts.

Tiger: Exactly. The policy-makers know that the "test-till-you–drop" concept has not produced results, and they are looking for educated individuals to lead Korea in the 21st century, not people who repeat facts without understanding them. So take a look at your lessons, and see how much they promote independence, originality, ethics, morality and democracy.

(More next time ...)

Discussion questions

1. What is the test-driven classroom?
    - What are its advantages and disadvantages?
2. What is norm-referenced assessment?
    - What are its advantages and disadvantages?
3. What is criterion-referenced assessment?
    - What are its advantages and disadvantages?
4. If you were the Minister of Education, how would you change the testing system?
    - Would you change the contents of the tests?
    - Would you change the type of tests?
    - Would you accept portfolios and projects as test data?

1) In Greek mythology, Sisyphus betrayed the secrets of the gods. His punishment was to roll a large boulder up a steep hill and to let it fall back down the hill from the top, and to continue doing this for eternity.

Socratic Dialog (4): The Classroom

Scene: Tiger is visiting Bear's house, somewhere in Korea.
Bear offers Tiger a piece of his wonderful apple pie.

Bear: Here you are, Tiger. I hope you like it. It's my grandmother's recipe.

Tiger: (*Accepting the piece of pie*) Thank you Bear. This looks delicious. I am happy to visit your home at last. You have made it very comfortable.

Bear: Thank you, Tiger. It's nice to have you here for a housewarming. I don't know what I'd do without a good friend like you to talk to.

Tiger: What's wrong, Bear? You sound upset.

Bear: You know how it is, Tiger. I want to do so much for my students, but I have to teach from boring textbooks every day and I have to prepare them for a national, multiple-choice test. There's no way I can introduce alternative assessment into my classes, not to mention humanistic teaching and learning.

Tiger: Don't worry, Bear. Your problems are shared by everyone. However, we have to look at the big picture. If we continue to prepare students for tests that no-one believes in, we must take responsibility for our non-action. As I've already mentioned, the official policy is about holistic learning, even if it isn't what actually happens in the classroom. Social commentators such as H.G. Wells tell us that "Civilization becomes more and more a race between education and catastrophe." This is a message we cannot ignore.

Bear: That's all very well, Tiger, but I'd lose my job if I tried to do what you are saying. Would you like another cup of tea?

Tiger: Yes, please, Bear. Your tea and apple pie are exquisite. It's so nice to relax here with you. Don't be so pessimistic, Bear. You would be surprised how many educators are asking the same questions. You don't have to wear a red headband and set fire to yourself. Just take a look at your lessons and ask yourself some questions.

Bear: Such as?

Tiger: Such as "How can I promote self-confidence, motivation and independence in my classes?" "What is the purpose of assessment?" "What does it mean to educate the whole person?" "How can the students take over responsibility for their learning?" "Why do we need teachers?"

Bear: Hang on a minute, Tiger. I need another slice of pie before trying to consume all these ideas of yours.

Tiger: Take your time, Bear. These questions will help you think about the meaning of education. I must congratulate you on your home. You have done a great job.

Bear: OK. Go ahead. I'm ready now. (*Putting another log on the fire*)

Tiger: For example, Bear, do your students know about their learning styles, learning preferences, learning needs, and long term goals?

Bear: Hmm! I don't think so. That's my job.

Tiger: Have you thought about the learning environment in your lessons? Is it non-threatening? Does it reduce anxiety and stress? Is it non-competitive?

Bear: Hmm …………………

Tiger: Let the students take responsibility for learning, Bear. They will thank you for it. (*Munching on another piece of pie*). Do they know how to reflect on their learning and how to assess their progress? Do they know how to set learning goals and then how to evaluate achievement? These are all doors that you can open for your students to walk through, and they will foster a love of learning that will facilitate motivated and informed study. Students who understand why they are learning will tell you what they need in the classroom, and your job will be transformed into facilitator of learning, language resource, "knower," guide and mentor. You'll be amazed.
(*By this time, Bear is happily asleep in his favorite chair. Tiger gets up and leaves quietly …*)

(More next time …)

Discussion questions

1. What is the role of the teacher in the language classroom?
2. What is the role of the learner in the language classroom?
3. What is the most effective way to teach language?
4. What is the most effective way to learn a language?
5. Is L1 learning different from L2 learning?
   - Please explain your opinion.
6. Is it important to teach learning strategies?
7. Is autonomy of learning important?
   - Please explain your opinion.

Socratic Dialog (5): Self-Assessment

Scene: Bear and Tiger are having a picnic on a river bank. The wind in the willows rustles the leaves gently, as three men in a boat (and a dog) drift slowly by. Bear and Tiger are lying on the bank. Bear yawns lazily and starts to get up.

Bear: Well, it's been wonderful talking with you and sharing your picnic, Tiger. I always enjoy our time together. But I have to get back and prepare the tests for Monday.

Tiger: (*Turning to face Bear*) Must you go, Bear? It's so quiet and peaceful here. Can't you make tests another day?

Bear: You're pulling my leg as usual, Tiger. Some things can't be ignored, however sweet the breeze, however inviting the water - though perhaps there is time for a swim before I go.

Tiger: Now, you're talking, Bear. (*They both jump into the river and swim about happily.*)

Bear: (*Floating on his back*) Don't you have to give tests as well, Tiger?

Tiger: Well, Bear ..., I don't <u>give</u> tests. I let the students write them. After all, the purpose of assessment is to let learners know what they need to do in order to improve their learning. They are the experts when it comes to assessing their needs and achievements.

Bear: Just a minute, Tiger, you're pulling my leg again. Are you serious?

Tiger: Of course I am, Bear. Self-assessment is one of the most important skills in life. Yet we rarely develop this skill in our students. When they leave your class and enter the wide world as adults, who is going to tell them whether they are performing as well as they should, or doing what is expected of them, or learning what they need to learn?

Bear: I'd never thought of that. I just test them and give out the grades.

Tiger: You're not alone in this obsessive testing culture of ours. We worship tests, yet we don't show students how to assess themselves. We just test-till-we-(or the students)-drop.

Bear: But what about cheating? Can you trust your students to be honest?

Tiger: Thank you for asking that question, Bear. Have you swum enough now? Shall we dry ourselves on the bank?

Bear: OK. (*They both climb out of the river and start to dry themselves*) But you haven't answered my question, Tiger. What about students who cheat when they assess themselves?

Tiger: As usual, Bear, this question reveals more about your assumptions and preconceptions than about the topic. <u>Of course</u> I trust my students. The first priority for me as, a teacher of human beings, is unconditional trust and respect for my students.

Bear: But ...

Tiger: No "buts" about it, Bear. It's quite simple. If you treat students like babies, they act like babies. If you treat them as adults, they act like adults. The freedom to self-assess is not a game or an easy option. It means being deadly serious about goal-setting, assessment of goal-achievement, and reflection on what needs to be done. When you show students how to self-assess, they become involved in the assessment process, they are respected by the teacher, and they are offered responsibility for their actions. Believe me, Bear, they will be eager to take on this responsibility, and they will thank you for giving it to them.

Bear: But ...

Tiger: If you put your students in a situation in which they see cheating as a suitable strategy, then you are to blame. After all, a genius is a lazy person. He/she finds simple ways of doing things that everyone else finds difficult. If you really don't want students to turn in the same compositions, then get them to work on different ones, introduce projects, ask each group to produce different reports. There are many ways of overcoming this.

Bear: But ...

Tiger: And in real life, "cheating" is normal. There are very few "new" ideas. When your boss asks you to make a report, you go to the Internet, you talk to colleagues, you read the relevant books and you summarize everything you can find.

Bear: But ...

Tiger: Remember, Bear, if you expect your students to be unworthy of your trust, they will act unworthily. If you expect them to be trustworthy, they will act in a trustworthy way. These are self-confirming predictions. Well, that was a lovely afternoon. I must go and have some tea. (*Tiger packs the picnic things and starts to leave.*)

Bear: But ....

(More next time ...)

Discussion questions

1. Is there any alternative to standardized testing?
2. Is self-assessment feasible in the language classroom?
3. Is peer-assessment practical in the language classroom?
4. What are the advantages and disadvantages of self/peer-assessment?
5. Can students be trusted to assess themselves?
6. Can students perform self-needs analyses?
7. How can we deal with students who cheat?
8. Should teachers be asked to do self/peer-assessment?
    - Why? Why not?
9. Should parents and students be asked to assess the teacher?
    - Why? Why not?

Socratic Dialog (6): Learned Helplessness

Scene: Spring is here. It is cherry-blossom time. Bear and Tiger are walking amongst the cherry and plum trees. Bear looks up at the trees, laden with blossom.

Bear: The blossom is so beautiful, isn't it Tiger? I love this time of year.

Tiger: (*Turning her face to the sun, which is shining through the branches*) Absolutely, Bear. There's nothing like it. The winter of our discontent[1] is over.

Bear: Are you making literary references again?

Tiger: Sorry, Bear. I couldn't resist it. (*Picking a sprig of flowers and sniffing them*) How are your students these days?

Bear: (*Frowning*) I don't know, Tiger. Things were going well, but after we had a mid-term test, they became unresponsive and lost interest. I don't know what to do.

Tiger: Don't blame yourself, Bear. This is one of the dilemmas of the present education system. However much we try to motivate our students to excel, we still have to prepare them for competitive tests which tell most of them that they aren't good enough.

Bear: (*Frowning even more*) I'm afraid you've hit the nail on the head, Tiger. No matter how much I help students to become excited about learning, I have to use the "Bell Curve" system which requires 20% of them to be "A" students, 30% to be "B" students, and the rest to be "C" or lower. It's depressing.

Tiger: I know what you mean, Bear. Imagine that you are an excellent teacher, which I know you are. You have motivated all your students. They are all learning efficiently and effectively. This is the best group of students you have ever seen and they all deserve A^+. However, because of the bell curve, some of these wonderful students must receive "C" or "D" grades. On the other hand, imagine a class in which every student is lazy and rude. Even though this is a terrible group of students, 20% of them must get "A." This is a perfect example of how education has been "sold down the river"[2] to the "number-crunching" needs of administration.

Bear: (*Frowning even even more*) But what can I do? I want to help all my students, but the ones who are not at the top of the class see no reason for trying.

Tiger: (*Patting Bear on the back*) It's time for tea, Bear. You shouldn't frown on a day like this.

Bear: (*Cheering up*) That's a good idea, Tiger. There's a nice café at the end of the street. (*They walk to the café and order tea and scones*).

Tiger: I had a friend once who taught Chinese. She told me that her department had the best teachers in the university, since all the students received "A" grades. I thought she was

---

1) Shakespeare: *Richard III.*

2) This idiom is a reference to slavery.

joking when I heard this, but imagine if it were true. We blame the students when they get low marks, but if we are excellent teachers, then all our students should get "A". Unfortunately, the system won't allow this to happen. After all, if we were able to educate everyone to a high standard of excellence, how would universities choose their new intake? Who would work in the fast-food stores or on the production lines?

Bear: (*Sipping a cup of Earl Grey tea*) This is delicious, Tiger. Have a scone.

Tiger: A big problem is that when we give tests, our students believe the results. They don't demand to see the criteria; they don't ask for item analysis; they don't criticize the basic principles behind the test; they don't ask to be tested according to their Multiple Intelligences. The test labels them as failures, and they believe it. They have learned how to fail. Even that wonderful class we were talking about would soon change after some norm-referenced testing. It was no accident that Einstein failed college.

Bear: Take it easy, Tiger. Drink your tea.

Tiger: (*Not listening to Bear*) We can't test autonomy, confidence, motivation, diligence, responsibility and other qualities. Yet we test everything else ad nauseam.[3)] You know what they say: "If it moves, test it." But we don't test for the things we really need, like social skills and teamwork. How about a corruption test? Let's make politicians take an anti-corruption course before they can stand for office.

Bear: (*Eating the last scone*) I know what you mean, Tiger. If only we could find a way of testing that did not label students as failures.

Tiger: You're right, Bear. There is hope. We simply have to integrate the tests with the instruction. We have to make tests which inform rather than discriminate. We have to find ways of assessing that help our students to become better citizens. We have to use portfolios, presentations, projects .... . Now, how about some tea?

(*Tiger pours some tea into his cup, and drinks pensively. Bear is sleeping soundly. Cherry blossoms fall gently on the two friends.*)

(More next time ...)

Discussion questions

1. What is the difference between relative and absolute assessment?
2. What is the difference between summative and formative assessment?
3. If every student has different learning styles and different Multiple Intelligences, is it fair to give the same test to every student?
4. What is 'fear of success'?
5. How can we develop self-esteem in our students?
6. How can we develop confidence and motivation?
7. How can we develop a positive attitude to learning?
8. How can we develop lifelong learning?

3) "Ad nauseam:" Endlessly, to sickness.

Socratic Dialog (7): Collaboration

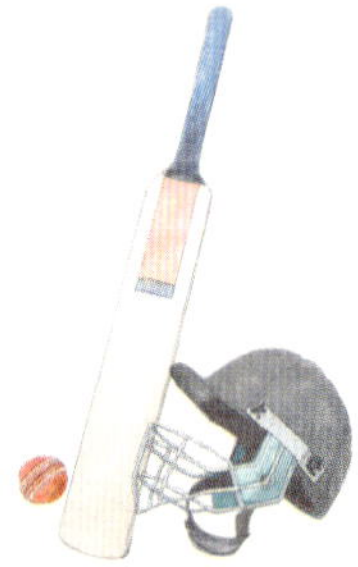

Scene: Bear and Tiger are watching sports on TV. Bear is very excited, and wants his team (the Worcestershire Bears) to win. Tiger is not so sure about this game of cricket. Tiger scratches her head and pulls her whiskers. She cannot understand Bear's excitement.

Tiger: I'm glad you like this game, Bear. I can't make head or tail of it.

Bear: (*Without taking his eyes off the TV*) It's quite simple, Tiger. The team that is out, or "at the wicket", is in, and the team that is not in, or "in the field", is trying to get the side that's in out. When someone is out, he goes in and the next batsman comes out to be in, until he's out, when he goes back in ....

Tiger: (*Turning to face Bear*) Yes, yes, yes. I'm sure it's quite logical. And what is the purpose of all this inning and outing?

Bear: To win, of course. Winning is everything. Isn't that the purpose of all sport?

Tiger: It might seem like it, Bear, especially with the professional Olympics we have these days. However, sport began as a means of promoting peace and brother/sisterhood.

Bear: HOORAY! (*Jumping up as a batsman is out and another comes in*) But we live in the 21st century, Tiger. Competition is a fact of life.

Tiger: Well ..., I agree that we are trained from the earliest grades to battle our classmates for grades and to see them as obstacles to our own success, but that doesn't mean that competition is desirable or even effective. The truth is that the majority of human interaction is not competitive but cooperative interaction.

Bear: Come on, Tiger. Stop playing devil's advocate.[1)] You know that competition motivates us to do our best.

Tiger: Actually, Bear, high level performance does not <u>require</u> competition; in fact it usually seems to require the <u>absence of competition</u>. Collaboration is a much more effective method of learning. Students at all levels benefit from collaborating with their peers. Even high ability students learn more when they collaborate with medium and low ability peers. As you know, the best way to learn something is to teach it to someone else.

Bear: HOORAY! (*Suddenly cheering, as the innings is over; the team that was in is out, and the team that was out is in*) I still say that competition brings out the best in us.

Tiger: Think about your students, Bear. They have to compete with each other for grades in an "I win, you lose" situation. This is extrinsic motivation. It has nothing to do with a love of learning. This is not bringing the best out in them. In fact, intentional competitiveness leads to lower performance, since trying to do well and trying to beat others are two different things.

Bear: Don't you think that healthy competition is good for building character?

---

1) "Devil's advocate": Taking the opposite point of view, even though you don't believe it.

Tiger: The problem is Bear, that competitiveness teaches most people to fail. People who believe they will lose see little point in trying, and they eventually believe that they deserve to fail. That's probably why some of your students are sleeping in class.

Bear: That's all very well, Tiger, but competition is unavoidable, and we have to learn how to live with it. I have to teach my students how to compete.

Tiger: I'm sorry to disagree again, Bear. The fact of life is that employers want collaboration. They don't ask a new employee "Can you work by yourself and beat everyone else?" They ask "Are you a team worker? Can you work responsibly with others?"

Bear: Oh, dear. This is very confusing. I've always thought that competition was good for us. At least it's the best way to have a good time.

Tiger: But people don't like losing, Bear, and in a competitive system, <u>most</u> competitors lose <u>most</u> of the time. Trust is also absent in a competitive situation, and you know how I value trust.

Bear: Surely you've heard the phrase "healthy competition"?

Tiger: In actuality, Bear, experiences in <u>cooperation</u> are the most essential ingredient for the development of <u>psychological health</u>. If you want to be healthy, collaborate! The greater the competition in any interaction, the less likely it is to be enjoyable and the more likely it is to destroy self-esteem, relationships, and standards of fairness. Why not play games that make us more cooperative, honest and considerate of others? The biggest gift you can give your students is intrinsic motivation ... the love of learning ...

(*Tiger continues, though Bear is engrossed in watching the TV, as the team that was out is in again, and the team that was in is out again, and the innings continue ...*)

(More next time ...)

Discussion questions

1. What are the advantages and disadvantages of competition?
2. What are the advantages and disadvantages of collaboration?
3. How can we teach collaboration?
4. Can we assess collaboration and team skills?
5. Is group work effective in language learning?
6. Are projects effective in language learning?
   - Are projects and group work practical?
7. "The best way to learn is to teach someone else."
   - Do you agree? Why? Why not?

Socratic Dialog (8): Journals

Scene: Bear is visiting Tiger at her school. He wants to observe Tiger's classes. Bear enters the staffroom. Tiger is looking through a pile of books.

Bear: Hello, Tiger. You look busy. Have you forgotten our appointment?

Tiger: Oh, Bear. Good to see you. Yes. I'm afraid it slipped my mind. Still, welcome to the school I hope you enjoy your stay.

Bear: What are you working on? Do you have to mark all those books? It looks like a huge task.

Tiger: Don't worry. These are student journals. I'm not marking them in the ordinary sense. I'm reading them and adding my own comments.

Bear: You mean the students write them ...

Tiger: That's right, Bear. Students write their own journals or diaries during the semester, and I make my own comments when I read them. It's a lot of reading, but it really helps me to get to know the students, and I can write things that are useful to them individually.

Bear: Don't you correct the grammar?

Tiger: That would take forever. If students want to concentrate on grammatical accuracy, I give them a Marking Code, and they mark each other's compositions. Students can do this very well, and it takes a lot of uneccessary burden off me. The grammar in the journals actually improves as the semester goes on. Regular writing improves by itself.

Bear: Interesting. I came here to watch your lessons and I've already learned something. But what's this diary here? The writing is more advanced than in the others.

Tiger: Thank you for saying that, Bear. That is my teaching journal. I like to keep a note of things that happen, and don't happen, in class. When I read about lessons that took place a few weeks ago, or even last semester, it helps me to reflect on my teaching and the students' learning.

Bear: What do your students write in their journals?

Tiger: I'm not strict about this. The process of regluar reflection and writing is more important than the content.

Bear: So you let them write about anything?

Tiger: That's not as simple as it sounds, actually, Bear.

Bear: What do you mean, Tiger? Do you mind if I help myself to a cup of green tea?

Tiger: Sorry, Bear. I wan't thinking. Please help yourself. There are some biscuits over there as well. Have you had lunch?

Bear: (*Bear pours a cup of green tea and takes some cookies*) Yes, thank you, Tiger.

Tiger: What was I saying? Oh, yes. It's not easy to come up with something meaningful to write about every week, so I let students write about whatever they wish. This also helps on a conseling level, since they write about whatever is important to them. When I read the journal, once or twice each semester, I can find out what is happening in their lives and what problems they are experiencing and I can offer appropriate advice.

Bear: I see what you mean, Tiger. Do you use any other types of journals?

Tiger: Yes. I sometimes ask a class to make a speaking journal. This is like a diary, but all the entries are verbal. Students use voice recorders, MP3 players, or even computers to record their voices every week.

Bear: I like the sound of that. Do you have any I can listen to?

Tiger: I'm afraid not, Bear. They are the property of the students, and I give them back once I have recorded my own comments on them. They are wonderful learning souvenirs for the students, so I like to return them as soon as possible.

Bear: It must be possible to have reading journals and listening journals.

Tiger: Of course. I've never tried them yet, but they make sense. Why don't you try?

Bear: I think I will. Thanks, Tiger. You have given me some good ideas already, and we haven't even stepped into your classroom yet.

Tiger: Speaking of which, Bear, it's time to go. The next lesson starts in five minutes. You can bring your green tea with you if you wish.

(*Tiger and Bear head off for the classroom. Bear takes a few more cookies and makes some notes on his wireless notepad.*)

(More next time ...)

Discussion questions

1. Have you ever kept a learning journal or a teaching journal?
2. Have you ever recorded your voice?
3. How can diaries be used in the language classroom?
4. How about pen-pals and key-pals (email-pals)?
5. What do you think of speaking journals?
    - Would they help with oral assessment?
    - Would they improve confidence and motivation?
6. What do you think of video journals?
7. Have you ever used drama to teach or learn English?
    - What are the advantages of using drama?
    - Can drama help with confidence and motivation?

Socratic Dialog (9): Performance Assessment

Scene: Bear is still visiting Tiger at her school. Tiger and Bear enter Tiger's classroom. Students are working in groups, looking at their portfolios.

Tiger: As you know Bear, it is portfolio conference day today, so students are looking at each other's portfolios and making constructive comments. Oh, good, they've already started.

Bear: Is this normal? Don't you tell them what to do at the beginning of the lesson?

Tiger: There's no need for that, Bear. Students have an assessment schedule in their portfolios, and they all know what happens today. Why should I tell them what they already know?

Bear: There must be some classroom management that you need to do.

Tiger: Not really, Bear. Students mark attendance in the Class Journal, and they also mark their self- and peer-assessment scores there. My job is to set up a workshop environment, fill it with learning affordances[1)] and then let the students get on with it. One of the best ways to motivate people is to give them real responsibility.

Bear: I see what you mean. And no charts of colored stars on the walls.

Tiger: Absolutely. That would be counter-productive and divisive. Everyone gets to put their work on the walls, and everyone's efforts are valued equally.

Bear: But how can you keep track of student work?

Tiger: It's all there in the portfolios, Bear. Different people work on different tasks, because they all have different learning needs. However, when I introduce a topic that I feel they all need to work on, I give them structured tasks, so that the people who need to spend a long time on the basic concepts can do so, while the faster students can work on more challenging tasks. As I said, it all goes in the portfolio, so I can monitor progress and talk to students about anything that comes up.

Bear: I like the idea of the workshop learning environment. No-one is sleeping, and everyone is on task. But how do you work performance assessment into this?

Tiger: That's a good question, Bear. You won't be surprised to learn that self- and peer-assessment are a large part of this. For speaking assessment, for example, I get students to assess themselves and each other when they are having a guided discussion.

Bear: How do you get them to understand the criteria for assessing oral skills?

Tiger: It's not as difficult as it sounds, Bear. Believe it or not, students can be more reliable in their assessments than many teachers. They are also responsible, sincere, and honest. I have no problem in asking them to acquire assessment skills.

Bear: How about reading and writing?

1) Opportunities

Tiger: You can see some writing assessment going on at the moment. In other lessons, students use criteria sheets to mark each other's compositions. Getting the students to mark accuracy and spelling allows me to look at the big picture when I look at their work. As for reading, I am just setting up an extensive reading program. I'm very excited about it.

Bear: You never stop, Tiger. How will you fit this into your lessons?

Tiger: I'm not too worried about that, Bear. I want to see what effect it has. There is evidence that regular student-directed reading, even without correction or comprehension activities, produces more efficient language learning than normal instruction.

Bear: Well, good luck with it. You have opened my eyes today, Tiger. I have often listened to you, but it's great to actually see this type of learning going on. I see what you mean about education of the whole person.

Tiger: Thank you, Bear. For me there is no other education.

Bear: I'm a little curious. When will you stop the lesson and talk to your students?

Tiger: Only when there is something that everyone needs to hear. As I said, everyone has an assessment schedule, the class assignments are on the web page, and we have a class noticeboard. Therefore most of the class management is taken care of. This allows me to talk to students individually, while the others are getting on with their work.

Bear: So you never say "Stop what you're doing and listen to me"?

Tiger: There is no need for such an autocratic statement. And remember, Bear, if we want to produce democratic citizens, we must teach them democratically.

Bear: And if we want peace in the world, we must teach peacefully.

(*The bell rings. Tiger and Bear head off for the staffroom for some tea and biscuits.*)

(More next time ...)

Discussion questions

1. What are the advantages and disadvantages of portfolios?
2. What are the advantages and disadvantages of extended reading?
3. What is "education of the whole person"?
4. What is a "workshop learning envirenment"?
5. What is "performance assessment"?
6. How can we teach democratically?

Socratic Dialog (10): Portfolios

Tiger and the Bear are on the mountainside again. They talk about portfolios, while looking for mushrooms. Tiger stops for a while and smells the air.

Tiger: Can you smell that, Bear? Isn't it wonderful?

Bear: What do you mean, Tiger? There's nothing here but leaves and trees.

Tiger: Exactly, Bear. Leaves and trees. And can you hear the waterfall in the distance?

Bear: (*Bear stops looking for mushrooms and listens for a moment*) You mean that rumbling?

Tiger: I love this time of year. Everything is so fresh, crisp, and clear. It makes me remember that everything is nothing, and nothing is everything.

Bear: It makes me remember that there's a cold wind on this mountain, and I need to get back and have some roasted mushrooms. I also need to prepare for tomorrow's lessons.

Tiger: Quite right, Bear. First things first. How are things these days?

Bear: Well, Tiger, I've been thinking about what you have been saying, but I can't see how it can be done. How can I bring autonomy, positive affect, emotional management, cultural awareness, social responsibility, et cetera, into my lessons? There just isn't time!

Tiger: That's right, Bear. While you see yourself as "the person who has to teach something," you will never have time for your students' development as human, social beings. But how many of your students have learnt what you tried to teach them?

Bear: Come on Tiger, that's not very fair. You know that it's difficult to measure learning.

Tiger: And you know Bear, that learners don't learn what the teacher teaches. So why are you still trying to force your students to learn the things that you want to teach them?

Bear: They have to know those things for the test.

Tiger: You can't keep using that excuse, Bear. You know that in a teacher-centered class, the best you can do is teach a few students in the middle of the proficiency range. For 30 percent, your lesson content is too easy, and for the other 30 percent, it's too difficult.

Bear: Can we talk about this on the way home? I'm dying for a cup of tea.

Tiger: Of course, Bear. How inconsiderate of me. (*They head for home*) Let's put it another way. What would happen if all your students were 100 percent successful?

Bear: If only! All my students would be able to get good jobs.

Tiger: And if all the students in Korea were 100% successful?

Bear: What do you mean? (*Bear and Tiger continue to climb down the mountain, carrying a bag of mushrooms.*)

Tiger: What if education suddenly became efficient and achieved its goals? What if everyone learned what they were taught? Would this result in a more desirable society?

Bear: Just a minute, Tiger. When did society come into this? Am I a social worker?

Tiger: You are an agent of social change, Bear, whether you like it or not. You are a role model for your students, and you are the epitome of your life-principles. It has been said that students don't learn lesson content – they learn the teacher.

Bear: Yes, of course. Lazy teacher, lazy students. Motivated teacher, motivated students.

Tiger: Right. But let's get back to the teacher-centered classroom. When you are teaching people what you want them to learn, the fact is that they can only learn as much as you.

Bear: What's wrong with that? (*Bear picks his way carefully past a large boulder.*)

Tiger: Your students need to go way beyond what you can teach them. Think of the technological advances in the last ten years. Then imagine the advances in the next ten years. Your students don't need facts, they need learning strategies. They also need to know how to manage their emotions in the hectic 21st century. They need to know how to reduce stress, deal with anxiety, solve difficult situations ...

Bear: But, Tiger, how do I give attention to these things? There isn't enough time.

Tiger: (*They arrive at Tiger's home.*) Here we are. There's no place like home. I'll get a good fire burning, and we can have some toasted portfolios.

Bear: Did you say "toasted portfolios," Tiger?

Tiger: Don't be silly, Bear. I said "toasted mushrooms." Have you thought of portfolios, though? They are wonderful for developing all the things we've been talking about. They are also great assessment tools.

Bear: I've heard of other teachers using them, but ...

Tiger: You can use writing portfolios, reading portfolios, or even integrated portfolios. They raise awareness about learning, they involve students in assessment, they use lots of self- and peer-assessment, they encourage creativity, they are a wonderful product of the learning process, they let students decide what to learn and how to learn it, ...
I could go on and on.

Bear: Before you do, Tiger, hand me that fork, and I'll start on the mushrooms. Is the kettle boiling yet?

Tiger: OK, Bear. You take care of the mushrooms, and I'll look after the tea.

(*60 minutes later, after the mushrooms have been consumed, and the two protagonists are sipping tea in the moonlight*)

Tiger: That was lovely, Bear. I love seasonal food – the right thing at the right time.

Bear: You've got a point, Tiger. We have too much unseasonal food these days. It's nice to gather the food and eat it straight away.

Tiger: By the way, you didn't ask me about portfolios. You must have at least three questions.

Bear: OK. Let's start with the obvious one. I'm an overworked teacher. Don't portfolios take too much time? Don't they simply increase my time management problems?

Tiger: This might be the case in the initial stages of setting up a portfolio environment, Bear, but as with self-assessment in general, portfolios can reduce the management and assessment burden on the teacher in the long run, in addition to giving much-needed meaning and responsibility to the students.

Bear: Really?

Tiger: Certainly. There are a number of ways to reduce the time involved. Let me see.
1: Give students clear information about the portfolios.
2: Make it a part of classroom routine to put entries into the portfolio.
3: Make students responsible for collecting information on a regular basis.
4: Identify items that go into the portfolio and list them on a form.
5: Share overall assessment through the use of Portfolio Conferences.

Bear: Fair enough. But how do we decide what goes into the portfolios?

Tiger: Is that your second question? Well, it's good to take things step by step, and to try different types of portfolio, different types of content, and different types of assessment. Make sure that you give a clear list of portfolio contents to the students. As time goes on, students will be ready to participate more in the decision-making, and the portfolios can become more autonomous and individual.

Bear: Hmm. This sounds very reasonable. But ... Well, my third question is one that you must be able to see coming.

Tiger: Let me guess. You want to know how to assess the contents of a portfolio?

Bear: That's right. If I'm going to use portfolios to measure affective, cognitive and social development, I need to know how to carry out that measurement.

Tiger: Of course. First of all, it must be stressed that portfolios are student-centered, and that they raise awareness of language learning and assessment. Because of this, it is important that they do not become agents of competitive assessment.

Bear: I know what you mean. This would just be "more of the same".

Tiger: Students can carry out regular self/partner/peer-assessments, and can have Portfolio Conferences. These help to foster collaborative, constructive, and non-threatening feedback. When teachers look at the portfolios, it should be with the goals of helping students to identify achievement, growth, and further learning needs.

Bear: Hurry up, Tiger, I'm getting hungry again.

Tiger: So portfolios are agents of positive attitude change, and the teacher must be aware of this. Asking students to evaluate each others' portfolios increases individual awareness of learning needs, without the teacher being involved. Instead, he/she can step back from micro-managing and review portfolios once or twice each semester, discussing relevant issues with individual students, and giving written and oral feedback.

Bear: Fine. You've convinced me. I'll think about getting some reading portfolios started next semester. Meanwhile, it's time for supper ...

(More next time ...)

Socratic Dialog (11): Rewards

Scene: It is a beautiful autumn day. Bear visits Tiger at her home.
When he arrives, Tiger is sitting outside, painting a picture.
Bear watches Tiger and decides to ask what she is doing.

Bear: Hello, Tiger. You seem to be enjoying yourself. What are you doing?

Tiger: Oh, hello Bear. I didn't notice you. I was so carried away. Do you like it?

Bear: Absolutely. I like the stylish brush strokes. Is this the "Sa-gun-ja" method that I've heard you talking about?

Tiger: That's right, Bear. Only four types of flowers are painted using this method. They are called "Mae-nan-guk-juk" and there are special ways of painting them. It's autumn, so I'm painting "Guk-wha" or chrsythanthemum flowers.

Bear: I didn't know you could paint Tiger, but you are very good at it. Have you ever thought of entering your paintings in a competition? I'm sure you could win a prize.

Tiger: Not really, Bear. I prefer to think that "The journey is the reward"

Bear: Isn't that a proverb? Is it the same as "The means is the end"?

Tiger: As Dr. Jonas Silk[1)] said, "The greatest reward for doing is the opportunity to do more." I paint because I love painting. It's very simple. I don't need prizes to tell me whether doing "Sa-gun-ja" is worthwhile or not.

Bear: I wish I could agree with you. However, I have to give prizes, or there wouldn't be any learning at all. Besides, I like giving stars when students do well.

Tiger: Perhaps you'll give me a gold star if I make a pot of tea. I have some Assam tea and some shortcake biscuits. Just right for this time of year.

Bear: Delicious! But don't you give rewards in your classes? It must be very boring for the students. Do they still want to do their best?

Tiger: I don't use the carrot or the stick, Bear. That is to say, I don't bribe students with rewards, and I don't punish them with threats.

Bear: So how do you show students that they are doing well, or that they should work harder? How do you deal with classroom management and discipline?

Tiger: My job is to motivate, Bear. If I can motivate my students to love learning and if I can involve them in every stage of the learning process, then they will learn whatever they want to learn, including the TOEFL, TOEIC and the CSAT.

Bear: You've said this before, Tiger, but don't you give any positive feedback?

Tiger: There is a difference between rewards and constructive feedback, Bear, whereas there is very little difference between rewarding and punishing students.

Bear: Really, Tiger? Are you serious?

---

1) The virologist, Dr. J. Silk (1914-1995), discovered the first vaccine against Poliomyelitis.

Tiger: Yes, of course. Just let me pour the boiling water into the pot. If you look at the ways we teach, you will find that we either say "Do this, or I will punish you" or "Do this and I will reward you." It's all about getting children to do what you want.

Bear: I think I'm ready for that cup of tea. You can certainly be surprising at times.

Tiger: Sorry to burst your bubble, Bear. Have a shortcake biscuit. You don't have to do anything to earn it, and I won't punish you if you take two.

Bear: So you are saying that rewards and prizes are a behaviorist method of manipulation. Don't they motivate people at all?

Tiger: Of course they do, Bear. <u>Rewards motivate people to get more rewards</u>. Think of your classes. When you say "The first group to finish gets a prize," what are you saying?

Bear: I am just trying to make the activity exciting and getting them to do their best.

Tiger: Do you mean that the activity is boring? Or do you mean that they wouldn't do their best if you didn't offer a reward? You are actually saying that speed is more important than anything else. People who take longer to understand are effectively being punished for their learning style.

Bear: Don't be silly, Tiger. Students love competing for prizes.

Tiger: Ask the people who don't get the prize. Do they feel motivated to work harder for the prize next time? Or do they just stop working? I'm afraid extrinsic rewards are neither necessary nor appropriate. The more children are rewarded to do something, the more they lose interest in whatever they had to do to receive the reward. For example, students working for a grade are less interested in learning than those who aren't graded. And those who receive frequent praise are less generous than their peers.

Bear: You've got a point there, Tiger. I think I <u>will</u> have another shortcake.

Tiger: Respect your students as human beings, Bear, and don't treat them as performing pets. If you want them to do their best, create basic motivational conditions in your class, and encourage positive self-evaluation. Remember - facilitation, not control. If you treat students as if they are already eager learners, then they can become eager learners. Let me give you a quote to think about on your way home. It's by Carl Jung: "The achievements which society rewards are won at the cost of diminution of personality."

(*Bear thinks on this, while munching another shortcake biscuit. Tiger returns to her painting.*)

(More next time ...)

Discussion questions

1. What do you think about giving rewards?
2. What do you think about giving punishments?
3. How can we promote intrinsic motivation?
4. How can we facilitate learning?

Socratic Dialog (12): The Internet

Scene: Bear has a new computer in his classroom. Tiger helps him to set it up. Tiger reads the manual, while Bear looks at all the parts on the table.

Bear: Well, I'm not sure what to make of all this, Tiger. What does the manual say?

Tiger: I can't help you much, Bear. There are all sorts of plugs, ports, plugins, connections, connectors, and parallel things that do something or other somewhere or other.

Bear: Maybe we'd better wait for the technician.

Tiger: I think that would be best. We could get things seriously wrong if we start messing around with things we don't understand.

Bear: I thought it would be simple. Just connect up, plug in, and off we go to the Internet.

Tiger: What are your plans for this computer, Bear? How will you use it in class? Will it help your students to learn English?

Bear: One thing at a time, Tiger. I know that you have a web page for each of your classes and that you use online noticeboards. I'd like to try some of these things as well. I'd also like to introduce e-mail projects into my classes.

Tiger: You mean getting your students to send e-mails to English speakers abroad?

Bear: Yes, but also to other English learners like themselves. I'd like to get the students communicating in English and learning about other cultures.

Tiger: Do you have any worries about finding suitable e-mail pals for the students?

Bear: I know that can be a problem, but there are some class-to-class keypal sites, and they take care of all the security problems.

Tiger: This sound excellent, Bear. Any other ideas?

Bear: There are all sorts of learning opportunities on the Internet and I'd like to use some of the great listening sites that are out there.

Tiger: This is very good. I hope everything goes well with your project. Now, if you'll excuse me, I can't wait all day for the technician. I'm off for a swim. See you for tea.

Bear: Goodbye, Tiger. See you later.

(More next time ...)

Discussion questions

1. How can we use e-mail projects in language teaching and learning?
2. How can we use movies and videos in language teaching and learning?
3. Is there any other technology we can use?
4. How can we use blogs and wikis?
5. How about online portfolios?
6. How about webquests?

Socratic Dialog (13): Bear Makes a Test

Scene: Tiger arrives at Bear's house. Bear is rather busy. Tiger stands in the doorway, looking at Bear.

Tiger: Hello, Bear. Are you ready?

Bear: Ready for what, Tiger?

Tiger: We have an appointment to go mountain climbing today.

Bear: I wondered why you were dressed up. Sorry, but it's out of the question.

Tiger: What do you mean? You're not turning down an opportunity to hike together?

Bear: I'd love to come, Tiger, but I've been up all night writing a test and it still isn't finished.

Tiger: I thought you had introduced classroom-based assessment into your classes.

Bear: Yes, I have. But the students have to have a test for the end of semester. The principal wants to see results in number form.

Tiger: Just a minute, Bear. You have been using student-centered, interactive, group tasks for a semester, and now you want to give your students a summative test? If your principal really wants to see results, show her the videos of your class and of the student performance projects. Show her students using the target language, talking to each other, and using higher-order thinking skills to solve language problems. Show her some student portfolios. If she can't see the growth that is going on, tell her she can't see the forest for the trees.

Bear: You know how it is, Tiger. Numbers speak louder than words

Tiger: On the contrary, Bear. As Einstein said: "Not everything that counts can be counted, and not everything that can be counted counts."

Bear: What do you mean, Tiger?

Tiger: Well, if you have to write a test, it must measure cognitive, affective and social growth, in addition to linguistic growth, and it must be based on everything that has happened this semester. If you just give a grammar-based test, it will be painting an inaccurate picture of the language learning and holistic learning that has occurred.

Bear: That's what I've been trying to do all night, but it's not easy. I know that high-stakes tests lower student expectations, they make schools into test preparation centers, they emphasize rote memorization and regurgitation of disconnected bits of information, they reduce academic rigor and dumb down genuine learning, and they cause stress and even sickness in the students. But I was hoping to make a test that would be different.

Tiger: I'm glad to hear that, Bear. I was beginning to think that you had given in to the pressure to teach to the test.

Bear: Don't worry about that, Tiger. I know the dangers of the test-driven classroom. I was reading today about a teacher who had been told to "stop teaching these kids to think.

They aren't going to do well on the test if you encourage them to make connections to anything except the test material." I don't want that to happen in my classes.

Tiger: So don't let it happen. Turn the test into a problem-solving, critical-thinking experience.

Bear: Wonderful. But how can I do that? Make it task-based?

Tiger: Yes, you could make some authentic, meaningful language tasks, but I was thinking of another approach.

Bear: What do you mean?

Tiger: Think of the principles of classroom-based assessment. How can we use those in a test?

Bear: You mean get the students to write the test?

Tiger: Right. This would be an exercise in teamwork, collaboration, critical thinking, decision-making, and any language function you care to think of. Students could make the test, take the test, and mark the test. What an amazing learning experience.

Bear: They could also find ways of introducing affective and social growth into the test. But what about the test-making criteria?

Tiger: It depends what you want, Bear. Do you want them to simulate a high-stakes test, or do you want them to reflect on the learning that has taken place over the semester? Do you want multiple-choice questions, or integrated, multi-skill language tasks? You will have to make this clear to the students.

Bear: You're right, Tiger. I'm going to try it. I wish you'd come last night. It would have saved me a lot of effort and frustration.

Tiger: Don't worry, Bear. No effort is ever wasted.

Bear: Let's go to the mountain!

(More next time ...)

Discussion questions

1. What is 'higher-order thinking'?
2. How can we assess problem-solving?
3. How can we assess critical thinking?
4. How can we assess language use?
5. How can we assess presentation skills?
6. How can we assess projects?
7. What is 'left-brain thinking'?
8. What is 'right-brain thinking'?
9. How can we promote curiosity?

Socratic Dialog (14): A Model Lesson

Scene: Tiger visits Bear's classroom and is impressed with what she sees. Bear greets Tiger at the school gates.

Bear: I'm so glad you could come, Tiger. I'd really appreciate your comments on my classes.

Tiger: (*Walking with Bear to the classroom*) It's my pleasure, Bear. I've heard interesting things about your classes these days. A little bird told me that you are practicing student-centered, classroom-based assessment.

Bear: Thanks to you, Tiger. You gave me all the ideas. (*Opening the door to the classroom*)

Tiger: And I thought you weren't listening to me when I rambled on. You surprise me sometimes, Bear.

Bear: Today is Reading-Writing Portfolio Conference day, so the students are assessing each other's portfolios. Would you like to talk with them?

Tiger: Certainly. But I'd like to ask you some questions first. How often do you have these conferences?

Bear: Three times each semester. Each student assesses 3 portfolios of other students, and has his/her portfolios assessed by 3 different peers each time. This means that each portfolio is assessed 9 times during the semester. This gives everyone a chance to get good ideas from each other.

Tiger: And what sort of things go in the portfolio?

Bear: Students can put whatever they like in the portfolios. If they want to include everything that they do in class, that's fine. Then they write "Collection Portfolio" on the front.

Tiger: And if they want to put only their best work in, then they write "Showcase portfolio"?

Bear: You've got it, Tiger. When we use supplementary activities, or when we do a project like a class newspaper, or a school survey, they can put those materials in their portfolios. Also, when we have group presentations, everyone assesses them and puts the assessment sheets in the portfolios. The main thing is that when they enter a piece of work, they have to add a self-assessment and a peer-assessment.

Tiger: I see. And how do you train the students to do this?

Bear: Well, we have a class website, with all the assessment sheets, assignments and assessment schedules on it. We also have an online noticeboard so that students can post presentation materials and remind each other about assignments.

Tiger: (*Tiger nods her head*) This is very good, Bear. And how do the students feel about this?

Bear: Why don't you ask them, Tiger? At first they were confused, but they soon got used to the idea of being involved in assessment, just as you said. Now that they know what is going on, they are happy to make their own portfolio criteria, correct errors in each other's work, and give constructive feedback to each other. They really take it seriously.

Tiger: (*Browsing through a portfolio that a student has given her*) Well done, Bear. Just think about it - you have given them responsibilities and opportunities they have never had before. But how do you give final grades? I know these are important to you and the students.

Bear: I'm very lucky, Tiger. The principal has agreed that I don't have to use a bell-curve in my classes. This means that I can really motivate my students. If they work hard, participate and show evidence of growth (cognitive, affective, and social development), then they can get A+. If they don't do their best, then they get a low grade, whatever their starting level. There are no easy rides in this class!

Tiger: This is very good news. And your students are used to collaborating?

Bear: They were uncomfortable at first. After all, their whole life has been about competition. However, they came to understand that cooperative learning is more effective than competition, and now the learning environment is much better. Students trust each other as well as trusting me, and they are happy to share their skills with each other.

Tiger: You don't do much talking from the front in these classes, do you?

Bear: You're right, Tiger. I feel like a real teacher now. I set up the learning environment, make sure that there are learning tasks for every level, and then I monitor and facilitate. I look for people who need help and I talk with them. This way I get to interact one-on-one with everyone.

Tiger: What can I say, Bear? You are doing great things. The apprentice has truly become the master! The teacher has become the educator! I am proud of you.

(The End)

Discussion questions

1. What is the ideal learning environment?
2. What happens in the ideal language lesson?
3. Talk about the ideal language teacher.
4. Talk about the ideal language course.
5. Talk about the ideal language textbook.
6. How can we make language learning enjoyable for all students?
7. How can we make language learning exciting for all students?
8. How can we make language learning challenging for all students?
9. How can we give one-on-one attention to our students?
10. What are our teaching/learning goals for the future?

English Reflections

An Interactive Learner Journal

First published 25 August 2004
Second edition 7 October 2010

Published by
Kyungpook National University Press

Address | 1370 Sankyuk-dong, Buk-gu, Daegu, Korea
Tel | (+82) 53-950-6741~3 Fax | (+82) 53-953-4692
E-mail | press@knu.ac.kr Website | www.knupress.com

ISBN 978-89-7180-299-1 93740